The Worst Girl Gang Ever

The Worst Girl Gang Ever

BEX GUNN & LAURA BUCKINGHAM

ONE PLACE. MANY STORIES

HQ
An imprint of HarperCollins*Publishers* Ltd
1 London Bridge Street
London SE1 9GF

www.harpercollins.co.uk

HarperCollins*Publishers*
Macken House, 39/40 Mayor Street Upper,
Dublin 1, D01 C9W8, Ireland

This edition 2023

1
First published in Great Britain by
HQ, an imprint of HarperCollins*Publishers* Ltd 2022

HB ISBN: 978-0-00-852495-1
PB ISBN: 978-0-00-852499-9

MIX
Paper | Supporting
responsible forestry
FSC™ C007454

This book is produced from independently certified FSC paper
to ensure responsible forest management.

For more information visit: www.harpercollins.co.uk/green

Printed and Bound in the UK using 100% Renewable Electricity at
CPI Group (UK) Ltd, Croydon, CR0 4YY

To all the baby loss warriors navigating their own shitstorm:
We know it's dark, but we've got you.

Contents

Introduction

*'**Being** alone can be lonely. But **feeling** alone when surrounded by others is perhaps the most isolating of all experiences.'*

If this rings true for you, then you have come to the right place.

Baby loss is like learning a new language and forgetting how to speak the old one. You can tell your story openly and honestly in a room full of people, but if no one can speak the same language as you, they won't understand. They will try; they might ask you to speak more slowly, or more clearly, but ultimately, they will not fully grasp what you are saying.

They may smile and nod, trying to look for common ground, or they might avoid you completely, finding it easier to ignore you than to struggle to understand what you are saying.

You might end up feeling as though you are boring to be around, like you bring down the mood. You feel that no one gets you and this new language is uncomfortable. You're not used to it either – it's hard enough trying to learn all the words yourself, let alone teaching them to anyone else. It's exhausting. And then you stumble across someone and you recognise a word or two… you realise that although you're both struggling a little to navigate the vowels, or articulate the narrative, you can actually understand one another.

This is us. This is our new language. It is the language of baby loss. It is a language built from pain, and it is a language we need to teach others.

Welcome to our gang.

Firstly, we are so, so sorry that you find yourself here. It really is the gang that you'd never choose to be part of, but, as you'll soon find out, this is also a gang chock-a-block with kind, supportive warrior women just like you.

There is a huge misconception that if your baby dies before he or she is born, they don't count. The experience is swept under the carpet because they never made it to the real world. But your baby doesn't just become real at the point of birth, they become real at the point of conception – and even before that, through dreams and hopes of motherhood. The point at which your baby dies during pregnancy has no bearing on the reality of your child. It is a life you've been planning and dreaming of, probably for years and cannot be measured in the days and weeks of gestation.

The idea of being a mother, for many of us, certainly comes years before we are in any sort of position even to contemplate having children. That's a considerable amount of time to think about something, to plan it, to allow your dreams to play out. So many of us have chosen names. We've pictured in our minds the holidays, the Christmases, the tiny little fingers, the schools, the cuddles… so in reality, the 'positive' on a pregnancy test – those two little blue lines – simply pull everything from years of daydreams into a new reality: a physical one. Is it any wonder, then, that when we miscarry, when we lose the baby that has been so settled in our hearts and minds since we were little girls, it is utterly devastating?

And yet we worry that we are not entitled to grieve. We worry that our grief is disproportionate to our loss.

We are here to tell you: it's not. When we experience this loss, we are grieving both the physical baby that won't ever make it into our arms, and the heart-breaking realisation that the world we have grown up creating in our minds, and believing in and trusting in, is not as we thought.

And ON TOP OF ALL THAT, we are expected to grieve quickly and quietly. To just 'get over it'. To not make a fuss. And not look back. And not make a big deal of it in case it makes others feel awkward. 'AT LEAST': we bet you've heard those loaded two words a few times! Some people will say things like, 'At least it was early,' or, 'At least you already have kids,' to try to make you feel better when, actually, it's bloody unhelpful, completely invalidates your experience and makes you feel you have no right to grieve. Well, you do! We all do. We at *The Worst Girl Gang Ever* share all these feelings and we have completely got you.

By picking up this book, you have realised the importance of sharing and making others aware of this very raw and very sad reality. According to our friends at Tommy's, the baby-loss charity, one in four pregnancies will end in miscarriage. One in four... That is a huge statistic. It's a huge proportion of pregnancies. So why do we not talk about it? Perhaps because it's too visceral, too private. Miscarried babies never breathed air or saw light; we don't have a language for them.

Fundamentally, it's a historic issue. It dates back to when things like periods, sex and childbirth weren't talked about.

And what about the 'twelve-week rule', what's that all about? Why do we feel that we have to keep our pregnancy a secret until then? Is it superstition? Will telling people cause us to miscarry? And will not telling people mean that we won't? Absolutely not. So why? Well, before ultrasounds became commonplace in the 1970s, it was the social norm to keep quiet until you started to feel foetal movements – or at least until you had missed a period or two. And talking about anything to do with our lady parts was strictly off-limits too. And even today, when successful campaigns are launched to raise awareness about female health issues – free sanitary products available in schools, for example – there is still a huge vacuum of information when it comes to the things women have to deal with. And stigmas are sticky little f**kers to break and change. It's time to smash the patriarchy!

But there is revolution in the air. It's our responsibility to pave the way so that future generations can be free of shame, judgement and isolation following baby loss. In Chapter 1: Dealing with Grief and Chapter 2: Marking Your Loss, feelings, emotions and the side effects of grief are explored. We want to empower women (and men) to feel able to grieve openly and talk about their experience without shame or judgement. There is some mega-useful advice on how marking and accepting your loss can be emboldening and powerful. And in Chapter 9: Educating Others, we open up the dialogue so that we no longer feed into that systemic problem. We want to equip women with the knowledge they need in order to manage their expectations.

We will also be exploring some of the most common and hurtful misunderstandings about miscarriage and baby loss, in an effort to educate and empower others. We'll go through some of the harsh, stark medical jargon to break it down and understand it. There is a great sense of liberation in understanding and not being afraid to take on the big words that often screen big emotions.

There is one horrible chapter on the Ugly Feelings (see Chapter 6) that we experience after baby loss or miscarriage, and we tell you now, it ain't pretty. But you know what? All the emotions that you have, they *are* pretty typical. Go ahead and flick over to that chapter now if you want to. We want you to remember one thing: YOU are not YOUR FEELINGS.

You'll be pleased to know that, as well as banging on about what we think on certain topics, we have also spoken at length to grief counsellors, mindfulness experts, relationship advisors, psychiatric nurses, and sex and body-love coaches who have armed us with a wealth of advice, guidance and practical tips to follow. We are hoping you might find this combination a) useful, b) essential and c) mind-blowingly reassuring. Introductions, websites and further information on those wonderful people can be found in our Resources section (see page 275).

We'd like also to point out that this book has been designed by us for you to read as and how you want. We've tried to keep the topics self-contained and digestible. We wanted to include our own experiences, exercises for you to try and honest advice in easily manageable chunks so that you are in control. It can be a pick-up and put-down source, one you can dip into when it suits you to reference a specific exercise from a specific chapter, or it can be a well-thumbed, cover-to-cover read to be savoured and shared. This is your guide, so use it however you want, whenever you want.

Our mahoosive thanks also go out to all the women and men who have shared their stories with us in a bid to envelop as many readers as we can in this gigantic hug of support and understanding. These personal, heart-breaking yet inspiring stories are sprinkled throughout the book so that relevant experiences are shared in the right way and at the right time. We could not have asked for a more positive response when we sent out the *TWGGE* signal (much like the Bat-Signal, but way cooler) and asked for help with this, showing that even in the darkest of times comfort can be given and received by those willing to share.

Many of these individuals have also been guests on our award-winning podcast, *The Worst Girl Gang Ever*. We've referenced particular episodes where applicable, so that you can have a listen to a contributor's full story if you'd like to. You will see notes such as '(S1, E4)', which refers to Season 1, Episode 4, to direct you to the relevant podcast.

WELCOME SQUAD

Right, before we go any further, perhaps now is a good time to introduce ourselves and tell you a bit about our own experiences. After all, you're in our gang now.

BEX GUNN

When I saw the two blue lines on my positive pregnancy test with my fourth child I breathed a sigh of relief. I'd done it. I had completed my family. As a teenager, I'd never had regular periods, and as I grew older they'd stopped altogether, so my fertility had always held uncertainty for me. I was fortunate to stumble across acupuncture early on in my journey to be a mother and was incredibly blessed with three children and no problems. So, when I saw that fourth positive pregnancy test, I thought I was on the home straight. I knew the 'loss' statistics but arrogantly assumed I was immune, having already experienced so many healthy pregnancies.

When I discovered that our baby's heart had stopped beating at my twelve-week scan, the bottom dropped out of my world and I realised how ignorant I was about the pain that miscarriage brings: the physical, the emotional, the psychological.

I was in hospital having tests and my husband brought in my laptop. I managed my pain through writing, and after I wrote and rewrote my experience I felt ready to publish it online. I sent it to *Metro* who published it. Laura read it, and she was one of literally thousands of women who wrote to me. But she stood out. She told me she wanted to go into battle with someone like me. Oh, and that I sounded like I had a hefty pair of lady balls, thus cementing our gang as being a place where a sense of humour is key. And so we began our mission.

When I compared our experiences, there was a part of me that felt unqualified to speak out, having just had one loss… but actually, I am *more* than qualified… I have made insensitive comments before, trying to help. I have invalidated the suffering of other women because I didn't understand it.

I get it now, and I can't bear the thought of women – *thousands* of women – suffering and feeling isolated in their grief, fearing the judgement of others should they choose to vocalise their experience.

When I lost our baby, I felt that, because no one talks about miscarriage, I wasn't coping and that my grief was disproportionate to my experience. Then I started talking, writing and sharing, and I found myself surrounded by women echoing my thoughts and feelings, it became clear that I wasn't as alone as I had felt – not by a long way. I knew then, with that realisation, that I wanted and needed to help others.

Our stories, whatever they may be, empower us as women. If we are given the freedom and support to own them, we will change the world.

Bex xx

LAURA BUCKINGHAM

Hi, gang,

They say one in four pregnancies end in loss, but for us it has been eleven out of twelve… and counting. Having been through chemical pregnancies, molar pregnancy, ectopic pregnancies, missed miscarriages and a heart-shaped womb repair, I feel like I've been on a bit of a roller coaster – or rather, stuck on the bloody ghost train. I've spent almost a decade immersed in this world and it's only in the last couple of years that I have felt less consumed by it – really since meeting Bex (but don't tell her that – she'll get a big head).

Experiencing baby loss in any form is an isolating place to be because of the misplaced shame that we feel and, of course, those poxy ugly feelings that tear us up inside (see Chapter 6). My 'journey' through recurrent pregnancy loss (hate the word 'journey', btw, but nothing else seems suitable) left me feeling so shit about myself as a woman. I hated my body, hated the world, resented others and I withdrew from everyone around me. Losing all faith and hope, I got lost down a deep, dark hole of self-loathing and paranoia. If you are there now, I see you.

It is through talking, writing and connecting with others who truly 'get it' that I have been able to heal a little. What we have created here at *The Worst Girl Gang Ever* is such a wonderful community, jam-packed with absolute warriors. If you've picked up this book for someone who has been through pregnancy or baby loss, THANK YOU for acknowledging the hell that we live through. If you have bought this book for yourself, you are now one of our gang. Welcome. We get you and we've got you!

Love Laura x

So, there you have it. We're just two passionate women brought together by baby loss and a common desire to help others. We know how devastating the experience is, and how isolated and lonely it can make you feel. Baby loss has a long-lasting, far-reaching effect on mental health and this is only exacerbated by the fact that we live in a society that is socially ill-equipped to deal with the pain it brings, so we marginalise it. But in doing so, we invalidate the suffering of women and couples. In *The Worst Girl Gang Ever* we want to say, 'It's time to change the things we cannot accept.'

Baby loss is a storm and we're all in the sea

As you begin your journey across the tumultuous waters of baby loss, you will find yourself in a little rowing boat, with a candle as your only light source. You have no choice about where you are thrown by the storm, and you wonder if you'll make it through at all. The waves are too big, too powerful, and you can no longer imagine the feeling of solid ground beneath your feet.

But you do continue, you have no choice – and as you get battered around by the weather, you begin to see the candles of other little rowing boats… As you get closer you see that some of these boats are bigger and stronger than yours; they have more passengers; they have maps and ideas.

You scramble aboard with your candle and you begin to share your stories; you realise you're not the only one in the ocean, you're not the only one suffering the storm, and as you talk and share, the sky gets a little less dark.

In the distance you hear the sound of whistles and shouts; there are lights – not candles or torches, but searchlights. It's a lifeboat and it's looking for YOU.

Once aboard, you sit tight with the other passengers, still bracing yourself against the storm, but with others there it's a little warmer, a little less frightening, a little less isolating.

The lifeboat motors away and, on the horizon, you see a ship. Though still stormy, it's no longer pitch-black – you get nearer and see hundreds upon hundreds of women with their candles. It's then that you realise you were never alone after all, you were just in the dark.

Too many women and couples feel as though they are in that little rowing boat. It's our job to find them and welcome them aboard our ship. We are HMS *TWGGE* and we welcome you with heavy hearts and open arms.

Chapter 1

Dealing with Grief

*'Navigating grief is like finding your way from Land's End to
John o'Groats with a map of France.'*

Anyone else feel like this about grief? It's like you know the basic
journey – you know that you're in Land's End and you know that John
o'Groats is a long, long way off. You know that's where you've got to
get to, but when you open your map, nothing makes sense.

We'll say that again. Nothing makes even a modicum of sense.
Nothing. At. All. You can't find familiar roads or place names… even
the shape of the country is different. And yet you set off, one foot in
front of the other. You start out in what you think is the right direction,
but before long you've got no idea which way to turn and your sense
of direction has completely abandoned you. You're exhausted and you
just want to be where you want to be. You don't want to be travelling
anymore – you can't face it.

Then you see someone in the distance. You stop to talk to them, and
they tell you which way to go, even if it's only for the next few miles…

but it gives you hope. You discard your map of France and you accept that you will get to where you need to be: slowly, surely, with friends and family and strangers helping and guiding you along the way.

You WILL get there, even though you expect a few setbacks. And asking for directions is a sign of strength.

You realise you will make it. And everybody's journey is different. Some find they get to John o'Groats quicker than others. It's not a race, of course, and this is the key to the journey. Everyone will have a different travel time, a different pace, a different route and a different way of navigating. We are here for you every step of the way.

> *'Take some time out to remember that, although our babies never made it home to our arms, they will always, always be safe in our hearts.'*

OUR DIFFERENCE IS OUR GRIEF

It's important to recognise that everyone's grief looks different. We cannot be judged on the way we grieve – if we are, then others may expect us to behave by their own standards and feel confused or cross when we can't. They may not understand why we struggle to come to terms with our loss. Perhaps weeks later we are still getting upset, while they would prefer to draw a line under our experience and move on.

Give yourself the time, space and platform to explore your grief. Speaking out to people who have been through a similar experience helps to validate your feelings, and this is the important thing here: You Are Not Alone.

When we lose our baby, our hearts don't suddenly empty – the love doesn't suddenly evaporate. It morphs into something else, changes shape and context, and what we are left with is grief. We grieve intensely because we love intensely. It's the same emotion, just on opposite ends of consciousness. So essentially what we are saying is that, if you are at all worried that you are grieving too much or for too long, remind yourself that it is just unspent love, and loving things hugely is a wonderful quality to have as a human being.

Why baby-loss grief is like no other...

When your grandmother dies at the age of ninety-five, you are left with lots of memories of that wonderful person. Memories are a hugely powerful thing, because you can locate those images in your head whenever you want and think about all the good times and experiences you had. Remember the time you wanted to run away to Granny's house when you were six because she would always give you chocolate ice cream for breakfast? The way she gave you a biscuit on a little china plate and let you win at Ludo... you get the idea. But when you have a miscarriage or experience early baby loss, you don't have the memories to fall back on. Instead, you are left with the memories you didn't make with your baby, the thought of all the things you will never get to do with them. So as well as losing your baby, you also lose the car ride home, the first words, first smile, first steps, first days at school, passing driving tests, getting married... You lose all those things in an instant. Because as soon as you see a positive pregnancy test you start to form those perceptions and you start to imagine what all those things are going to look like. And then it's all ripped away. Your brain can't locate the memories because there aren't any.

MOVING FORWARD, NOT ON

'If you lie in the water and hold your breath, you will sink. If you surrender and breathe steadily, with ease and purpose, you will float. See grief as the sea, let it hold you rather than consume you. I promise you will learn how to float.'

TAHNEE KNOWLES, THE MINDFUL GRIEF COACH

So often following baby loss, we are instructed to 'move on', and while we agree that it is important to recognise your experience and create coping strategies for yourself, it's important to understand that you are moving *forward*, not *on*. Baby loss isn't something we get over; we learn to live with it. These are the sentiments of Tahnee Knowles, the Mindful Grief & Pregnancy after Loss Coach, who we love for her ethos, her approach and her beautiful West Country accent. Tahnee uses mindfulness techniques to accept the spaces you occupy both physically and mentally, and to help you manage and adapt to these places. She lost her baby, Elvis Star, in labour at forty-one weeks plus six days. As a mindfulness coach she offers help and advice through the practice of being in the moment – acknowledging and accepting that while grief is undoubtably a tricky place to be, that is where you are. Over to you, Tahnee…

ADVICE FROM THE MINDFUL GRIEF COACH

Every woman will have had a different experience, and how they identify with that loss will be different, and so to anyone feeling the weight, I want to say this: when you feel the heavy chest, the lump in your throat, that you're holding back the hot and heavy tears… take a breath. Allow yourself to be held by grief. It is part of you now, but it doesn't need to consume you. Feel what you need to feel and breathe. Float to the surface. The weight won't go, but you will become better at carrying it.

RESPONDING TO GRIEF

This is about 'finding acceptance' and moving *forward*, not *on*. You can never move on from an experience like baby loss; you move forward with your grief, accepting all the emotions you will now feel. And not just the hard, ugly emotions either. You will be accepting of all the emotions you feel, so that if you go on holiday and you feel like a bit of weight has lifted, or you feel happy about something, allow yourself to feel that. It's so easy for the guilt to creep in. We don't always want to allow ourselves to feel happy or positive, because we are continuing life without our baby. So always keep in mind the sense that you are moving *forward*, rather than *on*, so you can allow yourself to have that light relief when it comes. And it will come.

People identify differently with their loss, which sometimes relates to the type of loss they've experienced or sometimes is just a matter of personal choice. For example, a woman who has experienced an early miscarriage might decide they don't identify with the idea of a 'baby', but they are still struggling with grief, while others will want to continue to bond with the baby they have lost. Elvis was born and died during labour; he was 10lb 6oz; he was very much a baby; he is our baby. I continue to mother him, and I continue building that bond with him. But sometimes I meet people who are about to disassociate and remove themselves from what has happened to them, and this can be a little bit different. Disassociation can creep up in various ways: the person might not directly relate things that go wrong in their lives, or physical symptoms or mental symptoms they are having, to the loss, so not dealing with it can potentially be quite difficult. But again, it's different for everybody. No one can tell you the best way forward – it's a personal choice.

SURRENDER TO THE CHANGING TIDES

'When you slipped away, a piece of my heart shouted,
"Stop! Wait! I'm coming with you…"'

After we experience baby loss, we're just not the same anymore and we often long to be back to our old selves. We ask, 'When will I be better?' 'When will I feel like I used to?' 'When will I stop hurting…?'

It's important to remember that you won't be the same person you were before you lived through this. And how could you be? It's completely life-altering.

Gone are your plans for the future; instead of a baby, there is no baby. The fingers of motherhood have loosened their grip and there is an emptiness in your arms and a piece of your heart forever missing. You will become a new person; you will feel things differently and act differently, and that's OK.

'Every child teaches you new lessons. That is no different with a child who dies.'

TAHNEE KNOWLES, THE MINDFUL GRIEF COACH

Losing a baby teaches us more than we would ever expect to learn. We learn that the person who we once were and the person we thought we would become are no more. We learn that we need to adapt in order to survive the pain. We learn that there's an alternative to the 'happy motherhood' narrative we were expecting, and we learn that we will now have to navigate this alternate path.

While we are on this journey, we can lose our identity. We find that we can't get back to who we were and yet we don't know who we are supposed to become. Give yourself time to get to know the new person your baby made you.

You are a continuation of them. The love you hold for the baby you lost is not wasted; it can be reinvested in yourself.

When there does come a time – a time when we feel 'recovered' – it will be with the acceptance that we are altered. We like to think of it this way: we can't go back to being the old versions of ourselves because there is now a little piece of our heart missing; the shape of it has changed and it beats a little differently. We're not exactly 'whole' anymore. Those little pieces of our hearts that have gone, have gone with our babies, for them to live in and listen to.

'We talk about them, not because we're stuck and we haven't moved on, but we talk about them because we are theirs, and they are ours, and because they will always be part of us. Because they will always be part of us. No passage of time will ever change that.'

SCRIBBLES AND CRUMBS BLOG

A 'me' moment

Grief is a tricky and uncomfortable place to be. Mindfulness is an acceptance that this is where you are. So, if and when you are ready, the Mindful Grief Coach suggests that you take five minutes to close your eyes, breathe slowly and fully lean into your emotions. As you do so, think about the following:

By accepting your emotions, you minimise any suppression, which isn't healthy.

Know that you can be happy and sad at the same time, and that's OK.

Be present. Try not to think too much about the future and don't dwell on the past. Embrace the here and now: this is where you are; accept it.

Don't rush to feel better; it will happen in its own time.

Allow yourself to smile. Allow yourself to laugh out loud. Your loved one who has left would not want you to be deprived of that.

'When we don't feel entitled to our grief, we bury it, and when we bury it, that's when the real trouble starts. And that's true in all walks of life; we bury our feelings in a bid to cope with the day to day and then, suddenly, out of the blue, for no good reason at all, they surface and they are bloody furious at being shut away.'

EXERCISES TO TRY

We love this collection of exercises from the Mindful Grief Coach, which can help us overcome the shittiest of shitty days. We'll just leave them here for you.

PRACTISE SELF-LOVE

Close your eyes, relax your jaw and drop your shoulders. Wrap your arms around yourself like you would your best friend, in a loving, warm embrace.

Breathe with ease and thank yourself for all that you are, knowing you are just right, just as you are. Breathe in feelings of love, and breathe out tension and upset. Repeat to yourself, either out loud or in your head:

'May I feel love.'

'May I feel peace.'

'May I live freely, joyfully and with ease.'

FEELING TRIGGERED? REMEMBER TO BREATHE

There will be times that grief will knock you off your feet when you are least expecting it. It can be triggered by a pregnancy announcement, or just watching siblings playing. When this happens, stop what you are doing and breathe. Breathe in through your nose to the count of four. Breathe out to the count of eight. Allow your heart rate to decrease.

Breathing in this controlled way allows us to revert from our sympathetic nervous system, which regulates our fight-or-flight response (when you feel uneasy, panicked, anxious), back to our parasympathetic rest state. Try it next time you feel triggered.

WALK WITH MOTHER NATURE

The first law of thermodynamics states that total energy is neither lost nor gained – it is only transformed. Sometimes getting out into nature is all the calm we need, and while it might not ease the pain, we can connect with the continuation of our loved ones in the world around us.

Hear them in the bird song.

Feel them in the wind.

See them dancing off the light in the horizon.

Let the warmth of the sun vibrate throughout your body.

'Grief is like living two lives. One is where you pretend everything is all right. The other is where your heart screams silently in pain.'

@WORDPORM, INSTAGRAM

EXPECTATIONS OF GRIEF

'Your baby will always be close, no matter how many yesterdays and tomorrows separate you.'

It is easy to feel as though you have gone back to square one when you have a bad day. It is also completely normal to panic that you're letting go of your grief when you smile, laugh or notice something beautiful about the world. The bottom line is… it doesn't matter how many yesterdays and tomorrows separate you and your beautiful baby or babies – because love doesn't work like that, and they are nestled safely in your heart forever.

'That huge event in my life when my child died may seem like a while ago for you, which might be why you don't check in as much or you expect me to be "moving on". What you might forget is that I am further away from a time when my child existed as a physical presence, and that pain is much deeper than the surface wounds you can see.'

TAHNEE KNOWLES, THE MINDFUL GRIEF COACH

In one way, we long for time to disappear, for the chasm of space between us and our experience to widen, for the jagged red scar on our hearts to fade, for the memories to soften and blur... We can wish to go to sleep for weeks, months or years and to wake free from the vice-like iron grip of our grief.

Time might be a 'healer', but grief doesn't get easier – you just get better at dealing with the injuries. You become more able to cope with everything that comes with grief because it has become your reality.

As time does pass, we feel ourselves moving further away from our baby. Our friends, family – even our partners – may move on, stop asking, wonder why we are down. Like any life-changing situation, the more you live with it, the more you find a place and a space for it. In the beginning your grief wears you – it's dominant and it's sharp and in focus – but it won't always be that way.

One day you will find it is the other way round; you are wearing your grief, like a faded badge that is comforting and familiar. At that point you will be able to revisit those thoughts and dreams with less pain, and it will become wonderful to think of your baby. The grief and the sorrow will always be there, but when it's softer you may be able to visit it with more fondness than pain. This journey of grief is not linear; we do not continue to get better and feel better every day – that's not how grief works.

One of the most traumatic elements of baby loss is the feeling that our babies won't know how wanted and loved they were. Sometimes it's so incredibly painful to think of our babies that we would rather not. We'd rather keep ourselves busy, and we'd rather avoid remembering those dreams we invested in so completely. In turn, this can make us feel guilty, like we are avoiding thinking of them, that we didn't love them enough.

We want to reassure you that it is because you love your baby so much that it is so painful to think of them. It is because, at the moment, life hurts so much without them.

We are sending so much love to you all.

'As far as I can see, grief will never truly end. It may become softer over time, more gentle, and some days the edges will feel less sharp. But grief will last as long as love does – forever. It's simply the way the absence of your loved one manifests in your heart. A deep longing, accompanied by the deepest love. Some days, the heavy fog may return and the next day it may recede once again. It's all an ebb and flow, a constant dance of sorrow and joy, pain and sweet love.'

SCRIBBLES AND CRUMBS BLOG

Someone is always missing...

'New dimensions of grief will continue to unfold as time passes and sometimes you can be caught off-guard with the thought that there will always be someone missing. If you become pregnant again after baby loss (see Chapter 8: Trying Again and Pregnancy After Loss), you might start to think about the fact that the baby you are carrying now will never meet his or her other sibling. There will never be a moment in time when all of your children co-exist, which is the reality for many who have children following the death of a child. It's a feeling of never quite being whole. Because every family get-together, every family photo, every family holiday and every family celebration, there will always be someone missing. So, while a new baby brings you hope, it's also a stark reminder of all the things your family will never get to be.'

TAHNEE KNOWLES, THE MINDFUL GRIEF COACH

Dear Griever,

There are no real words of wisdom we can give you; in fact, there's nothing that anyone can say to help you. So, sorry, this letter is, on the surface, pretty shitty and pointless. We just wanted to remind you that grief is a journey, and it is *your* journey; no one else can join you on this one. There are no right or wrong turns. There is no set path to follow and no real end to the process. The grief you hold will change in both shape and intensity. Sometimes, you will feel stuck in a time trap; the world will keep on turning and the same mundane things will keep happening over and over again, and most people won't even notice that your world has changed beyond recognition. There will be people who will bring light into your life and, gradually, the darkness won't seem as bleak. Remember, it's always darkest before the dawn… ('Shake it out, shake it out, ooh whoa'). You are a warrior – a fragile warrior, but a warrior all the same. And we damn well salute you.

With love,
TWGGE

THE BALL AND THE BOX

Having talked about how things will become easier over time, we think the 'ball and the box' analogy helps to illustrate this (and, as you probably already know, we love analogies at *TWGGE*).

The basic premise is that grief is like a box with a ball in it and a pain button on one side. To begin with, the ball is f**king massive, so it cannot move in the box without pushing the button of pain.

Sometimes this can feel suffocating and relentless, like you cannot survive. As time goes on, however, the ball gets smaller. It never disappears completely, and when it hits the pain button it is likely to be just as intense, but these instances become less frequent and you will find yourself being able to get through hours, days and weeks more easily.

There might be times, as you approach significant dates, milestones or events, when the ball inflates. During these times it is important to keep in mind that this is temporary – you have not taken a step back in your grief process.

This might be a useful analogy to help others understand the way you feel.

REAL-LIFE STORIES

We will be peppering real-life experiences throughout this book to put what we're talking about into context so that relevant experiences are shared in the right way and at the right time. One story that can be followed throughout the book is that of our friend Chris Binnie and his wife. We find Chris's honesty incredible. He verbalises so many of the unsaid emotions and feelings of baby loss in such an articulate way. Plus, he is so supportive of our community. He talks about his experience unashamedly and normalises the subject of baby loss with such simplicity and grace that when you speak to him you feel completely at ease. He is like the baby-loss 'dad' in our outfit, and we are like the bonkers aunts. Here is the first part of his story, and we have included the other parts later in the book so you can follow his journey.

CHRIS'S STORY, PART ONE

*'When you are in the hospital, in that bereavement
suite, you are in a bubble. And then you go back into the
outside world, and you realise that everything else in
that world is just carrying on as normal; that that world
doesn't realise the worst possible thing has happened.'*

My wife was high-risk because she has diabetes, and so we were
consultant-led all the way through the pregnancy, although there
were no concerns at any point.

My wife was booked for an induction at thirty-eight weeks
because of her diabetes and she got to thirty-seven plus five,
which was my last day of work before I started paternity leave.
She went up to the hospital that day (Wednesday) for a routine
appointment and quick once-over before Friday's induction and
for them to answer any last-minute questions she might have.

But a routine appointment then stopped being routine,
because there was no heartbeat. My wife had to ring me at
work to say I had to come home because our son, Henry, had
died. We were forty-eight hours away from everything being
absolutely fine. I couldn't process what was happening. There has
been a huge amount of progress in the way people talk about it
now, but back then, I came away thinking, 'Stillbirth? This doesn't
actually happen!' In my mind, you had your twelve-week scan
to check you could now tell everyone; and then you had your
twenty-week scan to find out whether you were having a boy
or a girl. Then you had a baby.

We are indoctrinated to think that we shouldn't mention we're
pregnant until the twelve-week scan because something might

go wrong, but once you hit twelve weeks, it's fine to tell people because everything is going to be fine. And then you tell people whether you are having a boy or a girl because you are on the home straight at that point. Despite my wife having diabetes, it never, ever crossed my mind that, beyond twelve weeks, anything could possibly go wrong.

Stillbirth is a real thing, and it still happens to people every day. I talk to a lot of professionals about bereavement care and when that starts, and I challenge healthcare professionals that whatever bereavement care they offer, whatever form it takes, it should start at the point of diagnosis, rather than when that family hits the hospital to go through labour. We were just left after being told Henry had died, not knowing what to do and how to process anything. We had to go home after the news. We had to close the door on the front bedroom that we had just finished decorating for Henry because we knew we weren't going to use it for that purpose anymore.

We went in on the Friday and Henry was born Friday evening. My wife had pre-eclampsia – she kept passing out and being sick, her blood pressure was through the roof, and I kept thinking she was going to die for quite a significant part of the later stages. I remember saying to the consultant at one point, back in the bereavement suite, that she didn't have to worry about keeping my son alive, all she had to do was make sure my wife doesn't die as well. I don't quite know how I found the clarity of thought to process it like that; it was very objective and rational. We had a couple of days in hospital, and you can't squeeze a lifetime into two days, so we just knew we had to make the best of it. And then we went back home.

When you are in the hospital, in that bereavement suite, you are in a bubble, you are protected from the outside world. And then you go back into the outside world, and you realise that everything else in that world is just carrying on as normal. All the silly things that used to wind you up are still happening. The world hasn't changed. But your world has. And that is challenging to process because you are thinking, 'This is the worst thing that has ever, ever happened to me and the world hasn't even noticed!'

Chris Binnie (S2, E11 and 12)

'I thought the worst was over, but I guess life and emotions aren't on any sort of schedule.'

CHRISSY TEIGEN

A word from Bex...

The hardest part of miscarriage for me is the fact that I feel left behind in my sadness, even by my husband. I feel that everyone has moved on – no one mentions it, no one even asks: 'How are you?' in that hushed tone reserved for grief anymore. I understand that people move on, I get it. But for me, it's slow and it's painful and I just want everyone to understand that when I'm down. It's *still* because my baby died and that is legitimate and fine and valid and normal. Because there is no expiration date on grief.

Bex

THE UNEXPECTED TRAUMA OF BABY LOSS...

Or, more simply, why miscarriage is so much more than a heavy period. Because let's be honest, shall we? Before we experienced it ourselves, we assumed that miscarriage was about sudden cramping and a heavy bleed; horrible, but overall a short-lived thing to be got over. So when it did happen, we were shocked to find that our view was completely skewed, and we were faced with the harsh realities of the loss: physical, mental and emotional. The trauma of losing one's baby is *not* an event that is got over, *ever,* let alone quickly. But due to the fact that, as a society, we don't and haven't been open about the grief it brings, we wrongly assume that everyone who has been through it has coped better than us, leaving us feeling shame, like a failure, on top of everything else.

We don't talk about this because no one talks about it. For too long it has been a taboo subject, shrouded in silence and misplaced shame, and because of this, culturally we lack the knowledge of how to support individuals and couples going through it.

We know things have to change. At the time of writing, there has been a call for the government to give women and their partners the legal right to take three days paid leave if a pregnancy ends before twenty-four weeks. Three days doesn't even scratch the surface (obvs) when you think about giving a couple long enough to come to terms with the loss of their baby, but what it would do is give them both a chance to catch their breath, to hold each other physically and emotionally in the total darkness of the early days. Experiencing baby loss through miscarriage is not an illness, and we should not be allocating sick leave to suffering couples, but instead validating their experience and suffering with dedicated, paid time off. This makes it real to the outside world; it gives the grief the recognition it has been lacking and so deserves.

Many of us grow up with unrealistic expectations of fertility and pregnancy, that as soon as we decide we want to start a family it will happen. Just like that. Our education on these topics has often been restricted to 'how not to get pregnant' rather than 'what if I can't get pregnant?', meaning when we reach our childbearing years, we can be unprepared for anything that deviates from 'normality'; we think of miscarriage as a rare occurrence, an extremely heavy period, a taboo subject that should only be spoken of in private and moved on from quickly with replacement babies and sighs of relief.

In fact, while the physical aspect of miscarriage is both brutal and traumatic, often it is not the blood loss or pain that haunts so many baby-loss sufferers. It is the other, more visceral side of things: the deep and frightening darkness we enter; the messy, exhausting headspace we occupy; the 'ugly' feelings we have and the shame that comes with them, and the confusion we feel as we wonder how valid our grief and sadness are and how long it is acceptable to feel them for.

A word from Laura...

I had this wonderful image in my head of Scoop, my husband, carrying our tiny new baby down the hospital corridor. The baby would be in its 'going home' outfit, all snuggled up in its car seat, and I looked forward to the day that this would become a reality. As a nurse working in a hospital, I was often faced with IRL examples of others doing exactly this. Day in, day out. It's so painful to watch your dreams play out in the lives of others. I would see people walking down that corridor and taking pictures of the momentous occasion; it triggered me every single time. When would it be my turn? Whenever I lost a baby, this corridor was always one of my first thoughts – we would have to leave the Early Pregnancy Unit after being told that we were no longer pregnant and make that walk, carrying a shitty leaflet about how to 'manage' the miscarriage instead of carrying our precious baby. It's another kick in the vag – this is grief after baby loss. It's a grief for future hopes and dreams that you never had the chance to make.

Laura

It's a lonely grief, and it's only those of us who live in this world of baby loss that truly get it. WE get you. We've got you!

When we lose our baby, we don't *just* lose our baby. We lose the ability to make our partner a parent, to make our parents grandparents. We lose our naivety, faith and the opportunity to enjoy future pregnancy because we no longer trust our body and we've lost confidence in ourselves and our society. We, as the mothers of babies that never came home, are changed women. We are different. Scarred. And… that's OK. Because while scars, at first, are ugly, raw and red, in time they soften and become paler pink. They tell a story. The story of you. And they will always, irrevocably, be a part of you.

Chapter 2

Marking Your Loss

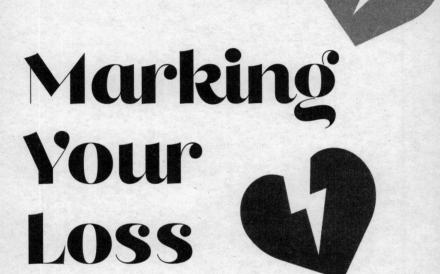

'I never knew how heavy emptiness could feel.'

The whole concept that a miscarriage is something you 'get over' invalidates every single emotion that goes hand in hand with it. When it occurs, we need to stop and think. We need to mark that moment in time and acknowledge that what has happened is important.

This was your baby, and they were so much more than a baby; they were a dream, dreamt when you were a child. A dream that gained momentum over the years. To sweep the loss of this under the carpet is wrong and goes against what every woman who has experienced it feels in her heart.

We create a space in our hearts, minds, families and households for this little life before he or she is conceived, so when we see that positive result on a pregnancy test, the reality of what we've imagined before just falls into place. Everything we have imagined for such a long time becomes our reality.

In order to honour our baby and our grief, we must first recognise that we are entitled to our pain. We must allow ourselves the platform and the space to grieve openly. Marking the loss of our baby with something tangible can help us to process, validate and acknowledge our little one and our experience.

DO WHAT'S RIGHT FOR YOU

One of our most frequently asked questions here at *TWGGE* is about how to mark the loss of a baby. And there is no right or wrong answer to this, because it will look different for everyone. It's about what feels right for you. It's about love. The love you have for your baby doesn't end when your pregnancy does, and if we fail to recognise this, we fail to recognise how human the experience is.

When our babies die, the unending love changes context and shape, but it doesn't go away. And that's why love causes us so much pain, because it's something we can't extricate ourselves from. Everyone who contacts us tells us how strongly they feel they need to do something, whether it's marking the day of your miscarriage or the day your baby was due. If it's something that you want to do, flipping well do it. And most importantly, don't be embarrassed or feel like you are wallowing in some unjustified grief. What you are doing is simply accepting that what happened to you was real. Your baby was real.

Validation

'My baby was: planned, was wanted, was conceived, was longed for, was loved, had a name decided, was thought about, had a heartbeat, shared my body, had a due date, had a first Christmas planned, had adoring parents, had a family to love them. My baby... existed.'

PRACTICAL WAYS OF MAKING YOUR MARK

How do you carry a child who isn't in your arms? It's so easy to mother a child who is here – it's so tangible, so practical… but how do you mother a child that isn't physically present?

When and how you mark the loss of your baby is incredibly personal, explains grief coach Tahnee Knowles. 'Be gentle with yourself. And if you don't want to explore this idea at first, then that's fine too. Maybe you'll come back to it when the time feels right. Or it might never feel right, and that's OK too. The ultimate aim of this is to bring yourself an element of peace.

'My continuing bond with [my son] Elvis is through meditation, but that doesn't mean that every time I meditate, I see him. Meditation helps me be at peace and continue to bond with him. Don't think that by moving forward in your life you are moving forward without them and that suddenly they become past tense, because that is not the case at all. You carry on their memory.'

There are numerous ways to mark your loss that might work for you, so go with what naturally feels right for you and your situation. Sending you all the squeezes we can on this one.

<u>Plant something</u>: There is something simplistically beautiful about directing our emotions towards Mother Nature during this time. Nature has a way of bringing everything into focus and providing a calmness, a gentleness. Planting a tree or buying a rose bush that you can visit on a regular basis is a wonderful way of marking your loss and making a connection. Here are a few tips to help you get the most out of the experience:

Do it yourself – planting your own tree, plant, seed or sapling is a personal project, and you might find that the therapeutic nature of having a hands-in-the-earth task to complete helps you focus.

Perhaps having just one spot to mark doesn't seem fitting for you; you might want to scatter a range of seedlings to create a wild garden area instead. If you love seeing bees and butterflies and insects visit and share your dedicated area, then perhaps this will work for you.

Many breeds of roses and plants have beautiful names, which you may find fitting. Watching plants flourish can be incredibly comforting.

Large pots to plant in are a great alternative if you don't have a garden or own your own home. You can take this wherever you go.

Every month has its own birth flower too. These could be pressed and framed as a subtle and personal way to mark your loss.

Bex's choice: how I marked my loss

My husband and I made the decision to bring our baby home following our loss. We wanted to bury them close to us, but we live in a rented house and the thought of one day having to leave them behind was torturous. So we went to the garden centre and spent some of our savings on pots and flowers. We created a patio garden outside the front door and buried our beautiful baby in that huge pot, under a rose called 'Sunny Sky'. The knowledge that our baby is snuggled up there is invaluable to me.

Bex

Get a tattoo: A symbolic and ever-lasting gesture, getting inked is definitely a personal and popular way of marking your loss. It's the permanence of a tattoo that can help us accept the reality, and the choices are limitless:

Words, names or beautiful scriptures might resonate with you.

Small symbols like stars, flowers or hearts in a place that only you can see might seem more fitting.

Numbers or dates that have significance are a simple but meaningful choice. Roman numerals as numbers or dates are popular.

Make sure you do a little word-of-mouth research and investigation when it comes to choosing a reputable tattoo artist.

Choose a keepsake: Keeping something physical with you can be a great source of comfort. This can be absolutely anything of your choosing that can be treated with love – a shawl, a cuddly toy, even an item of clothing. If it means something to you, that's symbolic enough. It can be kept secret so only you know where it is if you are in need of comfort, or it can be taken with you as a reassurance that it's always there. Having something tangible you can hug, touch and kiss – something symbolic on your bedside table, for example, that you kiss goodnight every night – can help bring peace.

Here are a few suggestions of mementos you may like to keep:

- Your pregnancy test – lots of women tell us that they keep the positive pregnancy test because the test was the first indicator of the reality of their baby's existence. Keeping this evidence resonates with a lot of women and we can understand why: it's a way of acknowledging and remembering that this happened and that your baby was real. Storing the pregnancy test in a memory box will keep it safe in a place where you can look at it and not lose it. It is worth mentioning that pregnancy tests do fade over time and that this might be triggering in a few years, so a photo of the test might be better (pregnancy tests do also smell of wee…)

- Scan pictures – this is a tricky one, as sometimes ultrasound photos are too distressing to look at or are refused at the time of the scan if the news is bad. We may forget to ask (understandably) or perhaps it didn't feel right to ask. However, it might be something that later on you wish you could have; an image of your baby, the sole picture of your baby, might later be something you desperately want to cherish forever. So how do you get one if you didn't ask? We can help here. Flick over to our Resources section where you'll find a template email to use if you can't find the words (see page 275). It is also worth noting that scan pictures will fade in sunlight, so take a copy or keep it in a box or stick in a book or journal to protect it from deteriorating over the years. Lots of love.

- Jewellery – often wearing a piece of special jewellery can help us feel close to our baby, such as a long necklace that hangs close to our hearts. There are many companies offering beautiful and commemorative jewellery, and you can choose something that is entirely right for you. Buying jewellery with your baby's birthstone is a personal and special way to remember your little one. You might find that something engraved with names and dates or initials is comforting. Alternatively, having something plain and simple that can be worn everyday (instead of being a 'statement' piece) might be more in keeping with your style.

<u>Write it down</u>: Writing can be both cathartic for you and helpful to others – if we feel strong enough to share our stories, that is. This is not just about making a memorial to your baby, but also about marking this period in your life. Diary entries when we were fraught teens in the throes of adolescence didn't necessarily produce any great works of prose, but recording and documenting our raw feelings and emotions is never to be dismissed.

- 'Free' writing is an exercise in simply putting pen to paper and letting your mind flow freely. Nothing you write has to make sense or look 'pretty'; it can simply be a way of channelling your thoughts, which can help process complicated emotions.
- Poetry is such an accessible form of communication. Short verses or longer, linear thoughts are a great way to mark your loss.
- Writing a blog is not only therapeutic for you, it can also help you 'find your people' and connect with others who have a shared experience (see journal prompts on page 58). If you're not yet ready to share yours, reading the stories of others can be a good place to start. It can help reduce feelings of isolation. And remember, there will always be a warm welcome for you on *TWGGE* social media pages.

<u>Charity work</u>: Many parents work with charities in memory of the baby they lost because it can help channel their grief, as well as provide focus, purpose and a legacy. If you feel you have a special kinship with a particular charity that has helped you in recent times, why not raise money for them when you feel ready? A bake sale or coffee morning will not only raise vital funds, it can also open up talking points with other warrior women looking for support. Sometimes setting yourself a physical challenge in memory of your baby can be beneficial. The training will provide focus, the exercise provides endorphins, and the act of physical work will aid sleep.

<u>Dedicate a day to them</u>: Making one day of the year a dedicated day for the baby you have lost is a beautiful and fitting tribute. This doesn't necessarily have to be an anniversary or a day that is more of a sadness trigger; it can be ANY day of your choosing.

- Make it a celebration – perhaps invite friends or family around to enjoy a special meal together.
- Mark the day – however big or small the event – as you would any other special day. Continue to dedicate this date to your baby for as many years as feels right for you.
- Here are a few ideas for that special day:
  - Turn off social media.
  - Spend time with loved ones.
  - Go for a walk in nature.
  - Visit the beach and write your baby's name in the sand.
  - Take time off work.
  - Go on holiday.
  - Light candles or hang ornaments.
  - Donate a gift for a child the same age as yours would be.
  - Make a cake (or at least eat one…).
  - Blow out a candle.
  - Don't put too much pressure on yourself. If you'd rather eat ice cream under a duvet, that's OK too.

<u>None of the above</u>: This isn't a tick-box exercise or a pass-or-fail test. Do what feels right for you. And if that means not doing anything, then good for you. There is no judgement in our gang, ever.

Laura's choice: why I haven't marked my losses

Hi, gang, I just wanted to share with you why I've never really done anything special to mark any of the anniversaries of our losses or due dates. It's probably because I have so many that it's just too much grief and sadness to deal with. I feel like I would be constantly grieving. Firstly, I wanted to reassure you that I've found in my experience, and from talking to others, the lead-up to the anniversary of your loss is often worse than the day itself. If I do remember I might go for a nice dog walk in the woods (my happy place) to get some fresh air because that always makes me feel a bit better.

Other than writing my book I've never really done anything to commemorate my losses – it just never felt right for me. In recent times I think I have realised why. After the first miscarriage I planned to buy a piece of jewellery, but I fell pregnant again – straight away (no period in between) – and lost that one too. So I never really had the chance to process the first one before I was dealing with it all over again. I felt like the original item of jewellery I had in mind was no longer relevant, as it implied there was one baby, but now I had lost two babies, so I didn't get it and then just never got round to it.

The more losses I went through, the less significant each one became, but my longing for motherhood became more significant – I was just desperate to be a mum, and following every loss I just wanted to hurry up and start trying again ASAP.

The long and short of it is that everyone must do what feels right for them because we are all different people, in different situations, with different experiences, and no one should feel under pressure to behave in a certain way or feel like they are doing it wrong.

Laura

'One day you will tell your story of how you overcame what you went through and it will become another person's survival guide.'

BRENÉ BROWN

WRITING ABOUT BABY LOSS

We wrote a bit above about how writing about your loss can be cathartic and helpful for you and others, but here are some more specific ideas to get you going if you're not sure where to start.

JOURNAL PROMPTS – WRITING ABOUT BABY LOSS

Often the hardest part about writing is knowing how and where to start. Here, we have come up with a few 'journal prompts' to get you focused.

1. **Write something to your teenage self about baby-making.** We all know that sex ed taught us nothing much of any use about making a baby, as it was based mostly around avoiding sexually transmitted infections (STIs) and how NOT to get pregnant. Not to mention the unrealistic expectations it gave us after having to put condoms onto bananas (or cucumbers, depending on where you are from). Have a think about what you would say to prepare your younger self for what might lie ahead. Be realistic but sensitive and kind.

2. **Write a letter to your baby.** Be they already here with us, gone too soon, never having made it to Earth or yet to be created.

3. **Write something to your partner.** Maybe it's something that you would like to give them once it is finished or maybe you'd rather keep it to yourself. Either option is OK. It's also possible that your partner might want to write a letter to you. Do whatever suits you, there is no pressure. The whole idea is based around processing our feelings and being able to make sense of all that goes on in our mind.

4. **Write something to your future self.** Write it, seal it and choose a date when you would like to open it. Maybe in one year, or when you have your next baby in your arms. It could even be a letter to yourself for Christmas Day. It's an emotional task but it should be quite therapeutic. So, get the tissues out, make a cuppa and let the words flow.

5. **Write a letter to your body.** What would you say to your heart, your brain, your uterus? OK, so this is a bit more 'out there' and might take you a little while to get started – but once you do, the words will flow.

6. **Write down everything that you do in a day.** What made you happy and what didn't? Is there anything that didn't make you feel good which you can do less of or not at all, or maybe just at a different time? Or can you share the load? Do more of what makes you feel good!

Sharing Laura's story

I was not ready to share my story immediately, but I found great comfort in writing it all down. I set up a blog and wrote as if no one would ever read it. I didn't hold back, and I think that helped me process the unbelievable grief I had locked away. A few months later, I felt ready and clicked 'share'. The messages of love and support that followed were overwhelming. My blog is now a published book, *It Will Happen*, and I have received so many messages from women living a similar experience who have found comfort and companionship in what I have written.

Laura

HAVING A FUNERAL

Neither of us has had to go through the challenge of planning a baby's funeral, but we know that many of you in this gang have. A lot of people we have spoken to found themselves at a loss as to where to get the right information, or they were given information at the wrong time (why does an information booklet get thrust into our hands at the shittiest of times?). The baby-loss charity Tommy's (www.tommys. org) has lots of advice on this, and below are just some ideas of how you can make the ceremony unique and special to you.

Make it personal:
The one thing to remember above all else when you are planning this day is that if it matters to you, you should honour that feeling. If playing a particular song or wearing a particular item of clothing rings true, that's all that matters. There is no right or wrong way. Our

list below is made up of ideas and choices other TWGGE folk have shared with us.

- Incorporate readings and poems (see below).
- Play music.
- Light candles.
- Make donations to charity in your baby's memory.
- Wear a colour other than black.
- Include letters in the coffin from family members.
- Produce an order of service.
- Take photographs.

<u>Scatter the ashes</u>: There are several things you can do with the ashes following a cremation that can honour your baby's memory:

- Scatter them in a place special to you (some restrictions apply – you might need a landowner's permission, for example – so please ask your funeral company for further information on this).
- Bury them in a memorial garden or at home.
- Keep them in a decorative urn.
- Use them to make a piece of jewellery (there are lots of specialist companies that do this if you do some research online).

POETRY AND READING SUGGESTIONS

We want to share with you a few of the poems that mean something to us. They can be read aloud, printed and tucked away or memorised but if they bring comfort, please feel free to use and share.

The Space That Fits You

Soul
Who visited so briefly,
My heart beat beside you
And we were one.

Now... now my body is alone, and weeps.
My heart –
Ours
Our hearts, our minds, our eyes
Cry
For you.

But we did have you.
Us
We gave you our name –
Your name
And our love.

And so,
Forever
In our days and in our knowing,
We will hold a little space
That fits you.

                              Trina Rollings (Bex's mum)

If You're Wondering Where To Find Me

If you're wondering where to find me,
I'll tell you where I'll be,
I'm in that in-between bit,
The space where sky meets sea,
In the whispers of the trees
And the edges of your dreams,
Close enough to almost touch
But slightly out of reach.
I'm in the moon and in the stars
But never really far
And always, always,
I'm inside your heart.

Catherine Prutton

Little Snowdrop

The world may never notice if a Snowdrop doesn't bloom
Or even pause to wonder if the petals fall too soon.

But every life that ever forms,
Or ever comes to be,
Touches the world in some small way
For all eternity.

The little one we longed for
Was swiftly here and gone
But the love that was then planted
Is a light that still shines on.

And though our arms are empty
Our hearts know what to do.
For every beating of our hearts
Says that we love you.

Unknown

Chapter 3

Misconceptions

'It does count and it is real.'

MISCARRIAGE IS NOT THE SAME FOR EVERYONE

Many of you will be all too familiar with the misconceptions that surround miscarriage. Often the experience of one person is assumed to be the same for another, but this is simply not the case. While some women experience a lot of physical pain, others may struggle more with the emotional toll. Some may find the trauma lies in the effect on their relationship. Some women already have children at home, while others may have been through cycles of fertility treatment. Each experience is entirely unique and will bring its own set of challenges and difficulties.

We are all individuals and, as such, every single experience we go through in life is felt and dealt with differently. These differences can be brought about by our upbringing, culture, philosophies, mental health, support systems, coping strategies… without even mentioning that we are all distinctive personalities with our own unique pathways and footprints.

Louise Taylor's story encapsulates this perfectly. We had a good giggle chatting to her for our podcast – it was like talking to an old friend even though we hadn't met her before. She was very open about her mental health and very honest about how the misconceptions and misjudgements around what happened to her – her own and other people's – made her feel. Not only was her story emotive, but her totally brilliant and upbeat attitude was thoroughly inspiring.

LOUISE'S STORY

'The worst thing was when people said to me, "Congratulations!"
That would make me feel really angry because I'd think,
"Why are they congratulating me when one of my
babies has died and one is fighting for her life?!"'

We found out at the twelve-week scan that we were having twins, and from that point on there were constant problems. It was a complete roller coaster, and we were scanned every week from twelve weeks. At one point we thought we were out of the woods when we were taken off 'specialist care', but then at the first scan after that we found out that there was only one heartbeat. I was just coming up to twenty-eight weeks and at that point I had to try to carry the other baby, my daughter Eva, for as long as I could, which was only another ten more days. One day before I was twenty-nine weeks she had to come out because things were starting to go wrong, and I needed to have an emergency C-section.

Eva spent nine weeks in NICU [Neonatal Intensive Care

Unit] and it was an incredibly lonely and upsetting time. It seemed like such a messed-up form of grief and loss because you have such mixed emotions... I had lost one baby and the other one was fighting for her life in NICU, so I couldn't be normal and just happy that I'd had a baby. The worst thing was when people said to me, 'Congratulations!' That would make me feel really angry because I'd think, 'Why are they congratulating me when one of my babies has died and one is fighting for their life?' I know they probably meant well, but it was such a hollow word to say.

The other biggest misconception a lot of people have about having a premature baby is that they assume it's just a little cute baby being kept all snuggly in a little incubator and all they need to do is grow and then they will come home. But it's literally life or death in NICU. Looking after a premature baby is really traumatic and intense, and you are constantly back at the hospital for checks. You are the odd one out in all the newborn baby groups because you have a tiny premature baby plus all the questions of why she is so small. I was convinced every other mum I saw pushing a pram had had a smooth ride and now had a bouncy, healthy full-term baby. I would hear them all swapping birth stories and moaning about swollen ankles in week forty. I would just be thinking, 'That sounds great to me!'

Then I had to explain that Eva was this age but she's not actually this age because she was three months early, so if you correct it she's actually this age, and then of course I was asked why she was so premature. I wouldn't always tell the whole story; it was exhausting and emotional. If I told the whole story or not would depend on my mood on any given day. The loss itself is strange because it doesn't make sense. When you are told you are having two babies, you are having two babies, and the fact that you came home with one doesn't make sense in your head. The biggest demon for me, still, is that twins exist in the world. I find that hard and that makes me feel so lonely. I just wished they didn't exist. If they didn't exist I wouldn't be reminded of it all the time. I can't get away from that, however hard I try. I have even convinced myself that other people who have had a baby haven't had it as bad, which I know is completely untrue, but it's an ugly feeling I sometimes get. My husband is much better at this. He can appreciate that no grief is better or worse, but for me, having a loss and the fact that Eva exists means that my grief is intertwined, and I can't close the door on it fully.

Louise Taylor (S2, E17)

It's very easy to write things off when it's uncomfortable to confront or even think about them. As humans, we are basically ill-equipped to navigate the pain of others, and never more so than where death is concerned. We find heartbreak desperately uncomfortable to witness, so we search our emotional filing cabinets for resources to 'make things better', but under the tab 'baby loss' there's nothing.

This results in a one-size-fits-all approach to women suffering with baby loss, which is not only inappropriate, it's damaging. It doesn't give us the space or platform to experience and come to terms with our emotions in our own unique way. We try to alleviate the pain of others with a kind of verbal emotional toolbox. We use it to try to patch someone up, but our approach to this can be clumsy, often resulting in the opposite effect to the one we intended, and we can end up smothering the person who's grieving with our words.

Instead, we need to try letting someone sit with their grief and saying to them, 'You know what? This is shit, I am so sorry. I will sit with you. You don't have to say anything, but if you do, I am here.' Just knowing that a person is really present and won't try to talk us out of what we are feeling or make light of those feelings because they make them uncomfortable makes a huge difference. It is the best thing we can do to help someone begin to navigate pregnancy loss.

Often, due to our discomfort, we will try to fill a silence or say something for the sake of it. A huge problem in modern life is that we strive to be happy all the time, but sometimes that's just not appropriate. Grieving is healthy. And mourning your baby and the life you were expecting to lead is a natural part of the healing and recovery process.

Trying to put an emotional bandage on someone who is suffering is invalidating. It is perhaps something that many people don't realise and won't fully understand unless they, too, have suffered. It doesn't need to be this way. We may not always have the right words to comfort a friend, family member or colleague who has suffered loss, but what we CAN do is be generous. Generous with our time, generous with our love and generous with our patience.

EARLY LOSS DOES NOT EQUAL EASY LOSS

This is such an important point for any early-loss mummas reading this… your baby existed and your grief is valid. When we experience early loss, at no point do we feel 'lucky' that our baby was only a few weeks old. We feel devastated. Heartbroken. Our little longed-for being won't be entering our lives and taking up residence in the world we had created for them.

Many of these comments, that we are 'lucky', are made as comparisons… but we absolutely shouldn't be making comparisons within baby loss. An early loss is a loss. An ectopic loss is a loss. A termination for medical reasons is a loss. A compassionate induction is a loss. A molar pregnancy is a loss. A chemical pregnancy is a loss. An IVF round resulting in a negative pregnancy test is a loss. These losses are all completely unique, all completely valid and all completely heart-breaking and grief-inducing.

When we experience early loss, we have the loss itself to deal with, the pain of knowing that the child we'd expected to bring home is never going to make it into our arms… and, if we didn't tell anyone about our pregnancy because we were waiting until the twelve-week scan, we might have the added pain of explaining to friends and family that we were pregnant, but we're not anymore. We might feel that society has written off our baby because he or she was an early loss, and this might make us feel like our grief and devastation is disproportionate to our experience and that our baby wasn't valid. Isolation comes from feeling that we have no platform from which to speak our experiences as we feel them. No understanding audience to share them with. No space in which to openly grieve. Well, here is your platform, your audience and your space.

It being early does not make loss ANY easier. And on top of the fact that our world has been turned upside down, we also have to deal with the stigma of our baby 'not counting'. But we want you to know that we know your loss was devastating and that your grief is justified. Your grief is justified.

*'Although physically my baby was small and my loss was early,
the world I had created for us was huge and lasted our lifetime.'*

UNPLANNED PREGNANCY

'Just because my pregnancy was unplanned, it doesn't mean it was unwanted.'
The whole idea that it might be a 'relief' if a miscarriage occurs following an unplanned pregnancy is ludicrous. Often couples who

experience unplanned pregnancies have to get their heads round things very quickly and make huge life-changing decisions to accommodate their new baby. Therefore, when they discover that their baby is not for this world they not only have the grief and physical pain to deal with, but the anticlimactic reality too.

This is a massive head-f**k. Especially if you might also have friends and family throwing in insensitive comments such as, 'Perhaps it was for the best,' or 'Never mind, you weren't ready.' This can lead to the sufferer torturing themselves with thoughts such as, 'Was it my fault? Did the baby think I didn't want it enough?' It's NOT your fault and it IS devastating. Sending you so much love.

*

The following people have all experienced an unplanned pregnancy. Have a listen to their stories. They all demonstrate that once you see those two pink lines, your heart expands to hold a baby, even though your mind didn't realise it was ready.

Megan (S3, E17) realised she was pregnant with an unplanned baby and despite the fact that she and her partner had been together for a long time and had plans to have a baby in the future, it took them a couple of weeks to get their heads around it. It was a surprise, but a happy one. 'We were excited – this is exactly what we wanted, just maybe a year earlier than planned.' She was diagnosed with an MMC (for a definition of a Missed Miscarriage see page 263) at the twelve-week scan.

Louise Powdrill (S4, E1) was in a new relationship and previously had a coil fitted when she found out she was pregnant during lockdown. It was unexpected and a huge shock for her and her partner, as they hadn't been together long. 'I remember doing the test and us both looking at each other thinking, "Oh no, what are we going to do? This wasn't planned." I was just starting to get my head round it at the point when [a miscarriage] happened. To go from that to one week later being prepped for emergency surgery and losing a tube, it was a total head-f**k!'

Rhys and Leila (S2, E21 and 22) fell pregnant with an unplanned pregnancy shortly after they met. Leila moved to live with Rhys and changed jobs too. When they went for an early scan at ten weeks they found out that the baby had stopped growing at seven weeks. 'There was a part of me that was trying to rationalise it by saying, "It wasn't the right time, we should probably spend more time together as a couple before we become Mum and Dad,"' says Leila, 'but we knew we were in it for the long haul. We were so disappointed and I felt like a fool' (page 138).

Ruth Corden (S3, E6) conceived during her honeymoon in 2013 but didn't realise until she woke up in bed covered in blood a couple of weeks later. She was told by her doctor that she'd been pregnant but wasn't anymore. She and her husband have not been able to conceive again since. 'I still look back and think about that baby.'

Becca Plant (S1, E4) fell pregnant when she lost her virginity. At the age of 16, when she miscarried, everyone around her was relieved. The only one who wasn't relieved was her. For more on her story, see her real-life extract later in this chapter (page 85).

A missed miscarriage is still a missing baby

The words 'I'm sorry, there is no heartbeat' are tattooed on the minds of so many of us. The shock, the feeling of claustrophobia – I remember the silence of the stifling scan room, and then a sound – a cry of raw, undiluted pain, instinctive and animal-like... the shock of the realisation that it was me, my noise, my pain.

In the days that followed, I felt really stupid. How could I not have known that our baby had died? Why couldn't my body keep my baby alive? What was wrong with me? And to be told in a clinical environment that you are no longer going to be parents as you thought you were is... Just. So. Shit.

Our baby had died two weeks before my twelve-week scan. I opted for medical management because it was the height of the pandemic and, instead of faffing about with more COVID tests and surgical procedures in a few days' time, I just wanted it over with. However, three rounds of medication later, still nothing had happened. I was fuming.

Not only had my body let my baby die, but now it was refusing to cooperate with the drugs. I couldn't even get this bit right. I had no idea what to expect, from pain to blood loss, and I was embarrassed – I was in my mid-thirties and felt thoroughly uneducated about my own body and too ashamed to ask anyone. The fear of what lay ahead climbed in on top of my yet-to-be-examined grief and sat heavily – and then, my saviour. I received a text from my mum that changed my entire perception of what had happened and the way I felt about myself.

'Tell your beautiful, brave body it's OK to let go now.'

From that moment, I was able to reframe the entire experience. My body hadn't let me down – in fact, my body was so desperate to be a mummy that she just held on.

Bex

THE THINGS PEOPLE SAY

It's important to remember that friends and family are the last people who would want to deliberately hurt you, which is why this is an important but tricky problem to address. It's about reminding people that we all feel things differently because we are all unique. Misconceptions and platitudes seem to go hand in hand, but it's worth remembering that a 'fix it' approach will do more harm than good. So, although we don't want silence, we do want recognition of the terrible situation we are in, as it is vital to our recovery. The words that are used need to be considered in order to be helpful rather than harmful.

Below are a few examples of what, on the face of it, seem like comforting words but are in fact very painful to hear following the experience of losing a baby. Later in the chapter, we've also put together a list of suggested 'alternative' comments.

*

'It will get easier,' or *'Time is a healer/you'll feel better soon.'*
Although this may well be true eventually, grief has no timeline. We are forever changed and baby loss shapes us. It is something that we learn to live with, rather than get over. When we hear these phrases, we can feel that you are trying to hurry along our process or that it is not acceptable to feel sad for any length of time. We will probably stop speaking to you about our grief because we will feel that you just want us to move on, and we can't.

'Just try and get on with things if you can – stay busy, don't think about it.'
No amount of keeping busy will take our minds off the fact that our baby has died and our future no longer looks the way we had hoped and planned. When we are advised to 'get on with life' we can feel silenced, like our pain is not appropriate.

'I know what you are going through… I felt the same when my dog died.'
You don't and you didn't.

'I was going to call/text/email but…' or *'I didn't want to visit – I thought you needed time.'*
We know how uncomfortable this experience is for others. We get it, but sometimes you just have to suck it up – after all, if someone else's reality is too painful for you to acknowledge, imagine what it's doing to them. Our baby will never be far from our mind, so if you are worried about causing further upset, don't. Ignoring baby loss is only going to increase the pain it causes.

'Stay strong!'
This old chestnut! 'Stay strong' is such a go-to phrase. It is meant as a compliment, because being 'strong' is so widely perceived to be a desirable trait. However, if we are consistently told to be or stay 'strong', then we feel we are failing when we struggle or feel 'weak'. We are in danger of feeling that we no longer have a platform to speak our truth and share our struggles.

*

Rebecca Dickson – Bexy D – knows first-hand how painful it can be when people say the wrong thing after baby loss, even if they're trying to help. She had a very similar experience to Bex and came from a similar family situation. We loved meeting her when she came on our podcast in Series 1. In fact, this was a chat that was filled with a lot of love and laughter.

BEXY'S STORY

"You're really fertile after you have a miscarriage." I got told that a lot. Who on earth would think that's an appropriate thing to say?'

We weren't trying to get pregnant when I found out I was. We had struggled to have our daughter – who is now four years old – and went to a fertility clinic and I was so happy when I found out I was pregnant because it was so unexpected. I booked myself in for a private scan at ten weeks because I just wanted to see our baby and know everything was all right. I went in, full bladder and ready, but I knew there was something wrong when the sonographer kept going over and over the same area of my tummy. There was no movement on the screen and so she said she would perform an internal scan, as perhaps I wasn't as far along as I thought.

After what felt like the longest time being scanned, she told me that she was sorry, but there was no heartbeat. And that there were two babies, twins, and they hadn't grown past seven weeks. It was the worst day of my life. It was heart-breaking. I can't even describe the grief from that day.

There is 'me' pre-miscarriage and there is 'me' now, and I am not the same person. I think my partner, Rich, would say that too. It's had such a long-term impact on us. I am very aware of the fact that I have a four-year-old and she's brilliant and I am so lucky to be a mum because there are so many women who don't have that child to make them a living mother. But I feel so guilty for my daughter and my partner that I am so wanting. I really want another child, but that feels like I'm saying, 'My daughter isn't good enough.' And that's not the truth at all! There are loads of layers of emotion to this – grieving the infertility, grieving the miscarriage, dealing with the fact that three of my good friends had babies within a month of when I was due and trying to be a good mum for my daughter through all of this.

I had a lot of people try to say things they thought would help afterwards. 'At least you can get pregnant,' was one, as well as the more damaging, 'You're really fertile after you have a miscarriage.' And I felt like replying, 'So, not only am I devastated and heartbroken that I have had this loss, but now I am putting pressure on myself because you have told me I will be able to knock another baby out right away?' I still struggle with this.

I did put pressure on myself that I would be pregnant again quickly, because in my mind we hadn't even tried for the twins and I fell pregnant. So when people told me I should be so super-fertile I had in my mind that everything would be fine. Obviously I would be pregnant again soon. But it's not happened, and that's been really hard. And when our new neighbours – who obviously don't have any idea about our personal circumstances – come out on a regular basis and see us with our daughter and say, 'Oh, you need to have another baby,' it just breaks me.

And these misconceptions don't stop either. I did a post on social media about my miscarriage about a month or so after it happened, and people think they can keep talking to you about what has happened. And while I do want people to acknowledge it, I don't want them to bring it up in everyday conversation when I am caught off-guard, saying things like, 'Oh well, at least you know your body can do it!' I actually hate my body. I have no faith in my body. I don't like looking at it. I don't look in the mirror because I am so angry with my body; in my mind, it hasn't done what it was supposed to do – when it came to my miscarriage – and it hasn't done what I wanted it to do since then.

Rebecca Dickson (S1, E12)

'AT LEAST...'

If you were to direct a sentence starting with the words 'at least' to anyone within the baby-loss community, you would be met with anything from an eye-roll to a snotty, mascara-streaked breakdown. 'At least it was early...' Has anyone ever felt comforted by this? You may have even said it to someone yourself before you joined the gang and fully understood the weight of these words. It seems laughable to us now that people can actually think this... why 'at least it was early?' Because you hadn't had time to form a connection? Because the loss itself wouldn't have been as traumatic? Because you shouldn't feel sad about it? We know people say these things because they want to make us feel better. But, please, anyone who needs to hear this, please don't try to put a positive spin on our loss. It. Just. Doesn't. Work. If you minimise the loss, the grief is doubled.

It is also worth saying that we will often try to reassure *ourselves* with the 'at leasts', but, just like slagging off your brother, it's fine for you to do it, but if anyone else jumped on the band wagon... Not. Cool.

*

Here are some of those 'well-meaning' phrases you might have heard as an early-loss warrior.

'At least it was early.'
Often this phrase comes after you have been asked how far along in your pregnancy you were when you lost your baby. And this can make you feel really shit, as you can start to feel that the validation of your baby was measured by gestation and that your grief should fall in line with that. Every loss is heart-breaking, no matter when it happens.

'At least you know you can get pregnant.'
Although the knowledge that your body is capable of pregnancy can be comforting to some, the fear of never being able to bring a baby home in our arms by far outweighs this. Women struggling with recurrent miscarriage find no comfort in the knowledge that they can become pregnant. The fear that pregnancy holds is crippling, because, for many, it has never led to anything other than pain and isolation. Knowing you can get pregnant is not helpful if you can't stay pregnant.

'At least it wasn't a real baby; it was just a bunch of cells.'
Similar to the 'At least it was early' remark (see above), somehow equating our hugely devastating baby loss with some science-y crap won't, we repeat, won't ever make us feel better. Being made to feel that our baby wasn't real is a heart-breaking systematic problem of this whole shebang. Your baby mattered, you matter – don't ever forget that.

'At least you didn't have the chance to get too attached.'
This is such a wild misconception because the world we want to live in with our babies is created with an abundance of love as soon as we decide we want to become a mother. So our grief and heartbreak and pain is valid because from the moment we see those positive pregnancy lines is often the time we become 'attached'.

'It wasn't meant to be.' / 'It was God's plan.'
Ahh, it wasn't meant to be. Well that's OK then, isn't it? We don't need to feel sad any longer now you have told us that. Bollocks. Telling us that our gut-wrenchingly horrible experience of baby loss was 'just one of those things, not meant to be' is something that will never not hurt. And hurting someone should never be 'meant'.

'At least you are still young.'
When babies are planned, we start 'trying'; we are prepared to get pregnant straight away, because that is, after all, what we learnt in school. If we are young, we have therefore decided that we want to become young parents. We're aware of our age – it was almost certainly part of our decision-making process. Being reminded that we are young can make us feel naive.

We're not going to rant about the above too much because we know that these comments almost always come from a place of love and warmth. However, they also come from a place of misunderstanding and a lack of education on how to show someone suffering after loss that their feelings are valid. Remember, when it comes to baby loss, THERE IS NO 'AT LEAST'.

> 'I've never understood the blanket secrecy you're supposed to apply to early pregnancy. It seems to me that pregnancy at any stage is significant and life-changing enough. Because losing a baby, a foetus, an embryo, a child, a life, is a shock like no other. You will watch your body backtrack, going into reverse, unpicking its work.'
>
> MAGGIE O'FARRELL

Rebecca knows only too well the trauma of early baby loss, as well as the misconceptions that can come from being pregnant at a very young age. She has had more than her fair share of grief, but she is a fighter. Our relationship with her started with hello and ended with us talking about vaginal dryness and how she was going to change the world with her new range of feminine health products. Here's a question:

if you saw a bottle of Femfresh in a mate's shower room, does she have a smelly fanny or not? Answers on a postcard.

REBECCA'S STORY

'I kept thinking, "What's wrong with me?" I was sixteen years old when I had an MMC and all you get taught in school is that when you get pregnant you then have a baby. I didn't realise miscarriage was a common thing.'

My fertility story starts when I was really young. I fell pregnant when I lost my virginity at sixteen years old. At my first scan, I had to give myself a chance to get my head around being a mum. When I had a further private scan it showed that there was no longer a heartbeat: my baby had died a couple of weeks after my first scan.

At that point, while everyone else was relieved, I was in turmoil. I had just got my head around being a mum and was coming to terms with it. I started to blame myself and thought, 'What's wrong? What has caused this?' I didn't realise this was a common thing. You get taught at school that you get pregnant, then you have a baby. I didn't cope at all. The worst thing was that people expected me to be happy [that I'd lost the baby] and I wasn't, so I bottled everything up. I was in a dark place. I felt guilty and I think I wanted to punish myself that this was all my doing and all my fault.

I had two more miscarriages before I fell pregnant with my son, Oliver, when I was nineteen years old. I was a young, single mum and Oliver was such an angel; he was so happy – the sweetest little boy. I still don't know to this day how he died, but he was in bed with me and he just stopped breathing. I called the ambulance and they took him to hospital, but they told me there was nothing they could do. He died a couple of weeks before his first birthday.

For the next couple of years I didn't cope. I would spend my evenings sitting by his grave. He was my world. I think it's the sort of thing that you don't ever think will happen to you.

I took part in some medical research where they collect the medical notes from a random selection of babies who have died with no explanation. I did this in the hope that one day I will get an answer, and because I want to feel like Oliver's death wasn't in vain. It will never bring him back, but I don't want anyone else to go through what I went through.

About a month after his funeral, I found out I was pregnant again and I was in terrific turmoil over this. But that was short-lived, as I then suffered a spontaneous miscarriage. It was probably the only time I felt some relief because I was still grieving Oliver so much, but, at the same time, I kept thinking, 'Why? Why is it happening again? I know I can have children, so why?' I had several more miscarriages after that and with my last one, during the procedure to clear everything out, I developed quite a nasty infection. The result of my infection is that I must now have a hysterectomy. I have had nine pregnancies in all: eight of them have been miscarriages (one of those was twins) and, of course, Oliver, who was my live birth. With my hysterectomy, I guess the future is set for me. I have had ten years of fighting battles; I am ready to fight back.

Rebecca Plant (S1, E4)

HELPFUL NOT HARMFUL

Here at *TWGGE*, we believe that the way to help women feel seen, heard and validated is to open up the dialogue and make these conversations more accessible. We are fed up with hiding behind airs, graces and social niceties and believe it is time to talk openly and frankly. When we can do this, people will start to understand that the way society has always taught them to deal with these situations is a load of old bollocks.

So, time to arm yourselves with thoughtful and considerate chat and move away from some of the well-intended but damaging phrases previously mentioned in this chapter. Instead, try some of the suggestions below:

KLAXON WARNING: This little list of gems is specifically if you are looking to help and support women who are going through or have gone through pregnancy loss and miscarriage. We're not immune to saying the wrong thing – we've been there, we've rather embarrassingly got the T-shirt by offering up some crappy 'silence fillers' before we realised how bloody insensitive our attempt at being sensitive was. But we can't beat ourselves up about the past. What we can do is learn.

'I don't know what to say, but I'm here for you.'
Honesty is the best policy – we know that finding the right words is hard. Letting us know you are in our corner is enough.

'I'm sorry. It's shit. I'll bring treats.'
Acknowledging how things really are instead of trying to make light of the situation is so validating – and treats are treats (i.e. always welcome).

'I am here for you if and when you are ready to talk about your baby.'
Knowing that you are a safe person to talk to and acknowledging our baby *as* a baby is, again, incredibly validating and will make us feel seen.

'I love you.'
Chances are, we are feeling pretty shit about ourselves and our abilities. We need reminding that we are loved.

'I am so sorry – I know how much you wanted this baby.'
Often following baby loss, we can feel that our baby didn't matter to anyone but us. It shows that you understand and recognise the importance of this little being and why it was so valuable to us.

'What a devastating time you are going through, I am so sorry.'
By recognising how horrendous our situation is, you are meeting us where we are, and that is – you guessed it – validating.

THE THINGS WE SAY TO OURSELVES

The concept of toxic positivity, of brushing miscarriage and baby loss under the carpet with a forced cheeriness and an 'oh well' attitude is not only invalidating in the short term, the mental health implications of it are both far reaching and long lasting.

> *'If you passed your driving test the first time, would you go back to the test centre to check if it counted?'*

The crux of the matter is that so many of us within the baby-loss community don't feel entitled to our grief, and there are many unsubstantiated reasons why this might be the case. We might have heard other people underplay our loss with toxic positivity, or maybe it's something we've told ourselves – either way, we need to smash the unfounded perception that we can just shake it off. Let's give you a big old *TWGGE* hug and get down to it – with absolute certainty and clarity.

You are right to be feeling the things you are feeling; your emotions are normal, valid, well placed and well proportioned. Often these platitudes of baby loss that we tell ourselves are really deep-seated fears, instilled by generations of 'stiff upper lips'. We may worry that we will be judged, that if we speak our truth about the depth of our pain, we will be labelled as an attention-seeker. So instead of doing this, we quickly follow our stories of misery and heartbreak with self-deprecating 'reasons' why we know our pain, our loss, is not as bad as it could have been. We have lived, probably for our whole lives, in a society where feeling sorry for oneself is unacceptable and self-care is viewed as an indulgent luxury. Well, it's not. Here's what you should remind yourself of when you start thinking any of the following thoughts:

'But I only had one loss.'
TRUTH: When our baby dies, it can absolutely rock us and our world. We've said it before and we will say it again: it isn't a one-time event, but a traumatic and painful experience that we will carry forever. We change. Our hearts change. Our paths change. Our views and our expectations all – join in with us now – *change*. Your grief is entirely valid.

'But I already have a child/children, so I should just be grateful for what I have.'
TRUTH: Baby loss is heart-breaking, whether you have children already or not. When we have children at home, we feel unbelievably grateful. Following baby loss, we hug them more tightly, kiss them harder, and we probably sit with them and watch them sleep, loving

every minute spent with them. However, the baby that we lost was made in the same way, with the same love and the same hopes for the future. When we choose to have a baby, it's because we want a baby – whether that be our first baby or to extend our family. Our stories and our grief are ours alone, and while we can relate to the stories of others, we cannot (and never will be able to) walk their path. Your grief is not misplaced.

'There was probably something wrong. I must accept that everything happens for a reason.'
TRUTH: Sometimes shit things happen for no good reason at all. At a cellular level there is a scientific reason miscarriage occurs, but there is also a scientific reason behind why cancer occurs. Would you ever say this to a cancer warrior? Of course you bloody wouldn't – so don't invalidate your own grief by dismissing it on these grounds.

'I laughed at a joke today – I must be fine.'
TRUTH: Just because you smile, doesn't mean you are over it. We hide our heartbreak with smiles all the time, sometimes because we don't want to cause others discomfort with our pain; sometimes because we just don't want to go into it; sometimes because life after loss is so f**king exhausting we'd just like to pretend that we are 'normal' for one moment.

If we have seen something beautiful or we've heard something funny or we've just found a little slice of happiness in our day, we shouldn't feel guilty. We aren't betraying our baby. Sometimes we worry that feeling better will take us further from our baby. We see the pain that rests behind these smiles, and we see you living with it. You are a warrior.

'It's just bad luck – I must keep trying.'

TRUTH: Having a miscarriage isn't 'just bad luck'. In fact, we're pretty sure that luck isn't involved one iota. Yet we can hear this phrase so often – even from various professionals – that we start to ignore that gut instinct. That sixth sense that perhaps there is a medical or underlying health reason.

Perhaps the first few times you tell yourself that you're a victim of bad luck you might get reassurance from it, as it might make it feel unlikely to happen again. But if it does, it might well leave you more pissed off than ever. So be honest with yourself. We need to be able to work through all the negative emotions we encounter and not just sweep them aside and replace them with less ugly ones.

'I will get pregnant if I stop trying so hard.'

TRUTH: We know that telling ourselves this is like telling someone not to think about Christmas when they see the Coca-Cola advert. When that ball is set in motion, that's that. But why wouldn't we 'try hard' when we want something so desperately? We are told to try our hardest in every other area of life in order to achieve what we want, so it's hard to tell ourselves not to try when we are desperate to do all we can to make a baby happen.

'It will happen when the time is right.'

TRUTH: We will tell ourselves this over and over again because it gives us a sense of fate or that the universe will help us in some way, but just not right at this very moment. However, it can make our trauma feel unimportant too. If someone said it to us, we would want to know what sort of information they had that we didn't about when the time is right! The thought that it *might not* happen is something we need to remind ourselves of; we need to respect that thought and acknowledge it.

'It's God's plan.'
TRUTH: This carries the same sort of sentiment as 'it will happen when the time is right', but with the added weight of religious connotations. You can believe in God and still find the situation completely heart-breaking. If you have a faith and this is still happening to you, it's doesn't mean that you will find it easier to accept or process. You are allowed to grieve the loss of your baby, however strong your faith.

'Why is patience a virtue? Why can't hurry-the-f**k-up be a virtue?'

Laura Gallagher has been on the receiving end of several of these unhelpful remarks – from herself and from others – during her conception journey, and she's heard a fair few 'at leasts' too. Laura is hilarious. She got in touch with us after she wrote her children's story *Robo-Babies* (see Resources, page 275), and she's a prime example of someone who doesn't sit in any one category, which can lead to all kinds of assumptions and misconceptions being made about her situation. She is now an expert on our Trying to Conceive course (TTC Course) and one of the most positive and passionate people you are ever likely to meet. And she's incredibly airy-fairy, which is another reason we love her.

LAURA G'S STORY

'Thinking we couldn't conceive naturally and using IVF to have my son was a total mind-f**k when I then got pregnant naturally twice and miscarried both times. People just don't understand that even though you have a child, that child doesn't cancel out the ones you lost.'

We had to have IVF to get my son Rafe, so I was under the impression that I couldn't conceive naturally and that I needed intervention. IVF is harrowing, exhausting, emotional and anxiety-fuelled, and there is a moment of joy when you find out you are pregnant, but it is instantly filled with dread. We only had one embryo; this was our only chance. But then I became pregnant and my son was born and it was this whole miracle of, 'Wow, we had this one shot and, wow, we are so lucky!' And I think that was my headspace for a year afterwards.

But I did feel guilty too because IVF happened for us the first time, and other people would say to me, 'Oh, you only went through it once,' with me screaming in my head, 'That was enough!' I was so terrified for the whole nine months because I thought, 'If I lose this baby, there is nothing else.' And it felt like I had held my breath for the whole nine months.

But then I found out I was pregnant again – it had happened naturally and it totally blew me away. It was an ectopic pregnancy and, to be honest, all a blur. It was a total mind-f**k because suddenly I was in a world I had never been in: the world of getting pregnant naturally. I was suddenly out of the IVF infertility world and into the world of people getting pregnant naturally and then, just as quickly, I was in the baby-loss and miscarriage world.

Nine months later, we got pregnant again and it wasn't such a shock that time and it felt like, 'OK, this is the right time.' But I miscarried again, and it felt like such a slap in the face, because I couldn't believe it had happened again. I know some people have many miscarriages, but I wasn't expecting even one natural pregnancy after having IVF, so to then have a second one – and to have that one end in miscarriage again – I was just so f**king angry. It was very early, but I believe once you find out you are pregnant, your whole life changes, and my son was going to be a big brother.

We told my family – we told them both times and when we went through IVF, because I thought it was important to share how we were feeling and for them to be involved from the beginning. But I was in this weird limbo – I didn't know who to identify with. I can get pregnant naturally, but I haven't been able to keep it, and I already have a son, which meant that a lot of people's automatic reaction to me was, 'At least you've already got one,' or 'At least you can do it naturally again.' And I would smile and nod and say, 'Yeah, yeah, it's so good, isn't it?' but I was so angry. I still am angry.

I still don't really believe that I can carry a child naturally. People have a misconception that once you have a child and once you've made it, so to speak, you won't be bothered! And in fact, it's harder as it goes on; it's worse, and that's something that I didn't anticipate would happen. With baby loss, it doesn't end – I'm still living it. I still feel so alone because all my friends are on their second and third child and I have to say to myself, 'I am so lucky I have my son, but I am allowed to want more.' And I am allowed to be sad about what happened.

I am happy I have a child, but I still have two experiences where two children were taken away from me. Having one child doesn't cancel out the ones you lose.

Laura Gallagher (S2, E9)

Amber Izzo has experienced something very similar. During her own struggle with IVF and baby loss, she found a general lack of understanding in those around her, despite their good intentions. But Amber is a bloody powerhouse! We just wanted to add a little note here to say how amazing we think she is for all the campaigning she does to end the postcode lottery of IVF treatment. She has put so much hard work in to making such important changes to help others, all while navigating her own experiences of infertility. Do have a little listen to our podcast episode with her (S3, E2) – we guarantee you'll fall in love with her, just like we did, rather embarrassingly, during the episode…!

AMBER'S STORY

'After my first cycle of IVF failed, I saw a change in my friendships; I was told it was "just one of those things".'

We knew IVF was our only way of conceiving because I had two fully blocked fallopian tubes, which have been removed, and PCOS (polycystic ovary syndrome [see page 265]), and we also have male-factor infertility. IVF was our option! We didn't tell anybody when we went through the first cycle; we were quite anxious about whether it was going to work and were probably quite naive in thinking it would work first time. We reasoned that we would be able to surprise everyone when it had worked.

In hindsight, it was very isolating because you are going through one of the hardest things you will ever experience, pumping yourself with all these artificial hormones, and your body is going through something so physically exhausting as well as mentally exhausting; all you really want is to be able to lean on people. When it didn't work and we told our friends and family, there was a real lack of understanding. Infertility is one of those things that, unless you are going through it, it's hard to comprehend just how difficult it is. When it doesn't work, you are in a grieving process and people don't understand that. I got a lot of, 'It's just one of those things,' and it was brushed off with a 'I am really sorry... but you can try again!'

It was just so dismissive of how painful it is, because of course you can't just 'try again' – trying again comes with all these different obstacles of further tests, further medical procedures, more money and more pressure on your body, your mental state and your relationship. I am under no illusions that when people say things like that it does come from a good place and they aren't trying to be insensitive. They just don't know.

I have a circle of friends who have researched IVF and what's involved, and I found that so beneficial because they then didn't have to always ask me lots of questions; they were aware of the process. If you don't know what to say, just say, 'Tell me what you need,' or, 'Tell me how I can help,' rather than a flyaway comment about the situation. If you feel uncomfortable about the situation, imagine how the person going through it feels. IVF is a complete roller coaster. You convince yourself it must work; you're injecting yourself numerous times a day, you range from insomnia to extreme fatigue, bloating – and that is just the physical aspects. It's a waiting game and you are just wishing the time away – then, when it doesn't work, you build yourself up for another cycle while processing why it hasn't worked, asking all these questions and blaming yourself for literally everything.

We live in Cambridgeshire, and they had removed IVF on the NHS the year before we needed it, so we weren't entitled to any NHS-funded IVF, despite the fact that it was a medical reason that had caused my infertility. We were one of three CCGs (clinical commissioning groups) that didn't offer any. It's such a postcode lottery across the whole of the country as to what is available; in some places you are entitled to three rounds and in other places it can be nil. NICE (National Institute for Health and Care Excellence) guidelines say you should get three fully funded rounds of IVF on the NHS [if you are 'suffering with infertility'], so I began the Fight for IVF Campaign and campaigned tirelessly for this. I started with Cambridgeshire, and in June 2021 they announced they were reinstating it. Now, couples living in Cambridgeshire are entitled to one cycle of IVF. We still have a lot of work to do, but it's a start.

Amber Izzo (S3, E2), Fight for IVF Campaign @fightforivf

PARTNERS AND MISCONCEPTIONS: WHY BABY LOSS IS DEVASTATING FOR OUR OTHER HALVES TOO

Very often during the horrendous experience that is baby loss, partners can be completely overlooked. That is, the attention is focused on the woman who is physically experiencing the loss, and while obviously the physicality of baby loss is experienced only by women, the emotional side of pregnancy loss and miscarriage is experienced by both partners. But we often find with men that the pain is shut away; they feel they have to 'keep it together' or 'keep strong' for their other half; they feel that if they can't keep a lid on their emotions, how can they possibly be the rock that their partner so desperately needs?

Seeing the person you love in untold amounts of pain – both physical and emotional – without being able to do anything about it, is crippling and debilitating and painful. What's more, often our partners *do* experience the blood loss and trauma because they can see what's happening – which is terrifying and, again, completely out of their control. Sometimes they have more of an awareness of what's going on because they're physically that bit removed from the situation.

Following the loss, our partners can be the doorway to the outside world. The one who stands alone in front of us, shielding us from everything outside our bubble until we are ready and then being asked, on a regular basis, 'How is she?' It can often seem that the importance is firmly placed on supporting and caring for the woman who has experienced the physical loss. So where does that leave our partners, who might feel that it's too selfish to say, 'What about me?'

Let's check in with them, and perhaps text a mutual friend to ask them to make contact too. The fact of the matter is, so many partners feel the pain of baby loss and they, too, want to grieve the little life they'd longed for. We should be sensitive to this and make them feel they have the 'right' to do that.

*

Laura-Rose Thorogood and her partner run the LGBT Mummies Tribe, a source of support for LGBT+ women and people on the path to motherhood or parenthood, and are huge advocates in their community. She knows first-hand how it feels to be a non-biological mother and the supporting partner in a baby-loss situation, and the emotional fallout it brings. We love her passion for supporting other people – it's unrivalled and blimmin' awesome.

LAURA-ROSE'S STORY

'Regardless of whether you're a non-bio or non-gestational parent, dad or partner – we all need support with loss.'

Becoming a mum is something I've always dreamed of. I always wanted four children – two girls and two boys. As a child, I didn't realise that my four-children family dream would be shared with a woman, yet after coming out fully at the age of twenty-one, here I am. Fast-forward to meeting my now-wife, moving in together, forcing her into proposing (the subtle hints always work!) and a marriage later, we made the decision to embark on the precarious path to parenthood – or motherhood in our case.

Once we'd decided who was going to carry first, we made the decision to go through a private fertility clinic. We knew it was going to be a bumpy ride, and even prepared ourselves for multiple negatives (my wife has severe PCOS [see page 265]). What we didn't prepare ourselves for was loss. A miscarriage. Loss of product. So many terms that felt so far removed from how we felt when we experienced ours. I say ours – my wife carried. But although I did not experience the pain or the physical scars, I carried the emotional ones in a way I did not know was possible.

Being a non-bio mother was something I hadn't really contemplated until that moment. To me, throughout our journey I was a mother, no less or more than my wife, even though she was carrying our baby. It was only at that moment and the ones that followed that I found myself 'othered', and I realised that I wasn't always going to be considered a mum, have my role validated or even be respected as one.

My wife was completely devastated that, after four rounds of IUI (intrauterine insemination), she had miscarried in her first trimester. The sheer confusion, discombobulation and shock on her face when she realised she was losing the baby – I'll never forget that crestfallen look when I arrived home to see her in the bathroom, crying that she had passed the baby. I remember so vividly driving to our local shopping centre to get her some new pyjamas and a dressing gown, numb from the shock that our dream had been taken away from her – from us. This was accompanied by guilt that I couldn't stop it happening, and the feeling of helplessness. A cascade of emotions followed – hope that the clinic had got it wrong, anger that it had happened to us and constantly questioning, 'What went wrong? What did we do?'

In the aftermath, what confused me was the way people reacted. I wasn't addressed by medical professionals and 'sorry for your loss' wasn't directed at me. How selfish was I to be feeling this way? But all the while, I was a mother too, and the feelings of isolation and invisibility made me feel like a bystander. Regardless of whether you're a non-bio or non-gestational parent, dad or partner, we all need support with loss. We may not physically lose the baby, but our hearts do. We need that support too.

Laura-Rose Thorogood, the LGBT Mummies Tribe (S2, E10)

*

While we believe that, from an emotional perspective, baby loss can only be fully understood if you've experienced it yourself, we truly believe that from an educational point of view, the support around baby loss *can* be taught and learnt. And because this behaviour *can* be learnt, it's our responsibility to do our homework and support each other as human beings. Being kind – to yourself and others – is always the right course of action.

Chapter 4

Isolation and Loneliness

'The privacy of baby loss should be a choice, not an instruction.'

We love a chat about privacy at *TWGGE*. We're always banging on about how important it is to find the confidence to break the mould and share your story, and to give others a voice to do the same. But something we also want to say is that, if you don't want to talk about your experience, that's fine too. If you're not ready, that's cool. If reading this or hearing what others have been through is enough to support you, that's absolutely A-OK.

Our point is that the privacy of your experience should be a choice – a choice you make and not an instruction that is given to you.

The privacy of something is dictated by the individual/s who have lived that story, and no one else has the right to make any decisions regarding whether or not that story is shared. We say this quite a lot. And we will keep saying it too. We're like an alarm that's running out of battery power – we are the continuing bleeping that will never be stopped. Our stories, whatever they are, empower us as women. BUT it IS and WILL ALWAYS be our choice as to whether we share them.

We have been directed by society for so many years to believe that anything involving our reproductive organs, such as puberty or our sex lives, shouldn't be openly talked about. These subjects are covered up with labels intended to make us feel that it's 'naughty' to talk about them or 'inappropriate' to share them: Too Much Information; crass; unladylike.

We believe this is a fight for the future of women. We don't want girls to grow up feeling ashamed of any experience their bodies and minds go through. We need to be actively encouraging them to share their thoughts, their concerns, their fears and their grief with us, because that is how we will all survive. By giving these emotions a voice, we can help women suffering through baby loss and/or infertility. We can give them words to read that show they are not alone in their thoughts. And if you are one of those readers who contacts us and says, 'I'm not brave enough to share my story yet, but I am enjoying reading other people's,' that's brilliant! You don't have to share your story to feel empowered. That's not what it's about. It's about the freedom to be able to speak out in a safe environment and without fear of judgement if you want to.

The difficulty with baby loss is that the subject has long been taboo and completely stigmatised. We are the first generation to really dip our toes into the water of open dialogue, and that can be scary and difficult – especially when we witness public figures like Meghan Markle or Chrissy Teigen being so publicly ripped apart for choosing this option. It doesn't really encourage the openness we so desperately need.

'Losing a child means carrying an almost unbearable grief, experienced by many but talked about by few. Yet despite the staggering commonality of this pain, the conversation remains taboo, riddled with unwarranted shame and perpetuating a cycle of solitary mourning. Some have bravely shared their stories; they have opened the door, knowing that when one person speaks truth, it gives licence for all of us to do the same.'

MEGHAN MARKLE

The good news is that we at *TWGGE* have lady balls the size of church bells and we are 100 per cent ready to shout as loudly as we can for all of us. And we'll be here if and when you want to shout with us. Just remember: your story, your choice.

FEAR OF JUDGEMENT

'Talking about baby loss is not attention seeking.' #smashthetaboo

One of our favourite messages (OK, favourite is slightly misplaced here, but you catch our drift) to drum home to all you brave warriors is that talking about miscarriage isn't attention seeking.

How many of you have felt, or been made to feel, as though you are attention seeking when speaking out about your baby-loss experience? We're willing to bet it's a helluva lot of you.

Often the fear of this is so powerful that it can prevent us from saying anything at all to anyone – and in so doing, we deny ourselves the platform to speak and the space to grieve. We become suffocated by the experience; it silently chokes us and when there is no outlet for this pain, it sits heavy within us and affects our mental health in the most negative way.

Historical loss

When I wrote about my loss publicly, before Laura contacted me and we set up *TWGGE* together, thousands of women reached out to offer me both their condolences and their stories. What struck me, to the absolute core, was how many of these women were no longer of child-bearing age. I had emails and messages from women who were in their fifties and sixties – women who had experienced loss more than thirty years ago and had held onto the pain of it since. Mostly, they started their stories with 'I've never told anyone this' or 'I was told not to make a fuss', and almost all of them, at some point, thanked me for sharing my experience because they felt that I'd given them permission to follow suit. Some explained that they were crying as they typed. These women had names planned and remembered their due dates. They felt that their grief had to be private, and in keeping it so their deep and painful wounds remained raw, not just for months, but for years.

Bex

ATTENTION SEEKING? SO WHAT??

'F*ck the ones who think we overshare…
your story is not for their benefit.'

This gets us, this really, really gets our goat… the ones who think we 'overshare' when we talk about our babies. Some of us have even been told this to our faces - we've been 'called out' on our 'oversharing'. Well… we're calling bullshit, because this comment, this opinion may just be the thing that prevents a woman or couple from starting their healing process. This Judge Judy behaviour can provoke silence through fear of being criticised or judged and can stop essential conversation, essential grieving and essential coping strategies being formed. When we deny ourselves the platform to speak and the space to grieve, we become suffocated by the experience. When there is no outlet for this pain it sits heavy within us and affects our mental health in the most negative way.

When it comes to talking about the loss of your baby, there is no such thing as oversharing - it is your story, and sharing it will not only help those with similar experiences feel less alone, it will provide others with a green light to talk about their own pain which, in turn, will not only help those with a similar experience feel less alone, it will provide others with a green light etc etc... do you see where we're going with this? The silence around baby loss is historically pervasive within society - but if we can turn this whole thing round and get the conversation around this subject flowing, we will have so much to offer the future generations as individuals and supporters. The thing is, the judgers, they're not important, and actually worrying about what others think can be crippling and debilitating. So we say 'suck our d*cks' to the ones that judge. Our stories aren't for you anyway. (sorry this is a bit ragey and a bit sweary, we've got our knickers in a right twist over it all...)

YOU BELONG HERE

'Baby loss can threaten your sense of belonging.
We've got you. You belong here.'

Grief and baby loss is absolutely brutal. Ain't no sugar coating that bad boy. But one of the more lasting side effects of grief that we've noticed and never expected is that it sort of robbed us of a sense of belonging.

When our babies die, we cease to belong in the category of 'expectant mother'. Our apps and the calendars we've downloaded and pored over become redundant and mocking. We no longer 'fit' with pregnant friends, with excited family members, with colleagues who are TTC (trying to conceive) or new parents.

We often feel that our energy will bring them down, so we avoid them, or they don't know how to adapt to our new status of bereaved mother, and so they (and there is no guilt trip aimed at them here) avoid us.

However you look at it, as we've said many times before, when our babies die we lose so much more than we bargained for, and this sense of carefree belonging is one of those many things. We are no longer sure where we fit in and that is hugely isolating.

But you are not alone. You belong here. With us. We know it's dark where you are, but we're a friggin' lighthouse and we see you.

*

Sally Linghorn knows exactly what it's like not to fit into a particular category, and feeling isolated as a result. She got in contact with us after experiencing an early loss and feeling invalidated in her grief. She found that our page and podcasts had helped and wanted to share her story to help others.

SALLY'S STORY

'I am in an invisible gang of people who have been pregnant this year but no one knows. You are just someone trying and it's not happening.'

When we started trying for a baby, I stopped taking the pill and after a few months I found out I was pregnant. I went for my first booking appointment and, to the student midwife's surprise, I wasn't overly excited about it. I just remember being extremely nervous.

I had seen things on the TV about miscarriage and one good friend of mine had lost her baby when giving birth, so I was quite closed and cautious. I probably came across as someone who had experienced loss before, whereas of course I hadn't personally; I was just nervous about the whole thing. I was probably a week or two away from my first scan when I had some light bleeding. I did lots of googling and I remember the fear setting in straight away – I would be religiously checking my knickers every time I went to the toilet.

I had found out I was pregnant the night before I was about to start working night shifts, as a vet nurse, and so after I started bleeding slightly there were several late-night upset calls to my husband during my shift and sending pictures of what I could see in the loo. When I had an emergency scan they thought the baby had stopped growing at seven weeks but there was a possibility that maybe things just hadn't developed yet, so we were in limbo. There was basically a period of about three weeks where I had to have multiple scans. Then one morning I had quite a substantial gushing of blood and contractions for a few hours. A few days after that, I passed something a little bit bigger. I had to have a D&C procedure [dilation and curettage procedure, to dilate the cervix and remove the endometrial layer] under anaesthetic, which pretty much broke me. I spent weeks in tears at home in my pyjamas, and that's when we told my family that I had been pregnant but had miscarried. We hadn't told them that I was pregnant because we were so cautious, and we wanted to get the first scan out of the way.

I have had some counselling, which I felt was the best way to go because, for me, it was all-consuming (and still is, very often). I was constantly phoning the Miscarriage Association or Tommy's to ask questions about why it happened, as I was on a continual mission of desperate fact-finding. I found out I was pregnant again around three months later, on my husband's birthday, and yes, we were super-happy, but again super-cautious too.

The bleeding started happening again around the same time and I remember being in tears at work, waiting for my night shift to end so I could go to A&E. A few scans later, we were told I had miscarried again. They let me take a genetics test, which revealed that there was a duplicate pair of chromosomes and that this was the cause of that pregnancy failing, and, after some further genetics tests, we found out it was a completely sporadic incident. We found out it was a girl, too, and the nurse who phoned to tell us the result knew how completely distraught I had been when we had come in. I couldn't face that bloody place again, but we had to go to that same ward: the same unit with all the pregnant women; the same scan rooms. I couldn't stop crying and it just felt never-ending. It's completely all-consuming.

I keep thinking, 'A year has passed now, I should have had a baby a few weeks ago.' I stopped doing night shifts, partly because of the association of such a bad experience, and I started a new job. But the job is in a female-strong environment with two pregnant girls, and I find it really hard to know how to react to them. It just makes me think, 'What about me? I have been pregnant twice, but I have nothing.' But it's so hard to communicate that. It's like I am in an invisible gang of people who have been pregnant this year. But you are not a pregnant person who needs to be nurtured, you are just someone trying and it's not happening.

Sally Linghorn (S3, E4)

KEEPING THE FAITH

Experiencing baby loss can test the very strongest of faiths. Those with a faith can question what the event means and why we have been put through the pain. Some find comfort in meditation and prayer, while others enjoy the community and love of a church family. (For more ideas about meditation, see Chapter 6: Ugly Feelings.)

The kindness of strangers

At the point of my miscarriage I had only just joined a new church three weeks previously. The news filtered through the church group and every day for ten days my husband and I had a meal delivered to us, cooked by people we'd never met, during the uncertainty of the first COVID lockdown. Having one less thing to think about was invaluable and to be shown such love and support by relative strangers was incredible. It made all the difference in the total darkness of those early days.

Bex

Dannika Agyeman has experienced loss after loss after loss and yet she keeps going. And not only that, she keeps sharing what she is dealing with in order to support others within the community. Her faith, although tested, remains strong.

DANNIKA'S STORY

'More times than not, it's just "unexplained". And the least scientific thing someone can say to you, which is said quite a lot, is "it's just bad luck", before you are told to "keep trying".'

When I was taught, like most girls growing up, how not to get pregnant, I wasn't ever told what can go wrong when you do want to have a baby.

When I had my first three miscarriages, I was referred to the recurrent miscarriage unit and more times than not they don't find a reason why you are having miscarriages. That's unless you're really lucky – and I say 'lucky' in a sense that you have an answer! More times than not, it's just 'unexplained'. And the least scientific thing someone can say to you, which is said quite a lot, is 'it's just bad luck', before you are told to 'keep trying'.

So I found that the only way I could get more information was to keep researching and talking to people myself. When I stumbled across various forums, chats and social-media communities, I found the help invaluable. The wealth of women sharing what they are doing, what information they have found out, what books they have read… it all helped me when it came to my own fertility journey. It gave me ideas of questions to ask and helped me advocate for myself when I had appointments. I felt more empowered too. No one goes around talking about their fertility struggles, so it's like, where do you go when you have an issue? It's these little communities that are amazing. The support aspect is amazing, but the information aspect is invaluable.

If you know there is a problem, you want to find a solution, and I am lucky that I am someone who knows how to read a research paper, for example. But I have also had to learn a lot, and the point being is that the more you know, the more questions you need to ask.

We did a test for natural killer (NK) cells [see page 265], but they didn't find any issue at that time. But then I realised there had only been a very small number of tests on my immune system. So we did some more tests two years later and found that my NK cells were high, as were my cytokines. Cytokines are immune markers that contribute to inflammation in the body, which are not good for sustaining a healthy pregnancy. I have pursued all these tests that I wouldn't have known existed had other women not shared their stories. We also tested my husband's sperm and he was found to have high DNA fragmentation, and again, the idea for that came from endlessly scrolling on forums. They don't routinely test a man for recurrent miscarriage issues, only when there is a problem conceiving. We also went down the IVF route, although we couldn't do it on the NHS because I was getting pregnant, but the point was we wanted to test the embryos because with high DNA fragmentation it was possible that the embryos we were creating weren't normal, which can lead to miscarriages.

My faith has kept me going. It's horrible to go through this, but feeling like I am not alone and to look in the Bible and see that even thousands of years ago there were all these stories about women who had problems conceiving and God has come through for them… it was helpful to draw on that. Prayer and meditation have helped me too, kept me sane. Even listening to worship music or having a bit of prayer time – I always feel better doing something rather than nothing.

Dannika Agyeman (S2, E6)

'How are you?' versus 'How are you... really?'

We've all asked someone how they are in a casual, almost flippant way, not expecting a full and honest response, haven't we? It's like it has been instilled in us at a young age. Whenever a grandparent would ask this question, the automatic response would be, 'Very well, thank you,' until the teenage years, of course, when nodding and grunting reigned supreme. If, though, we answered this question with anything other than a conditioned response, it would floor the person asking the question. So why do we bother asking? Herein lies a subtle tweak that can make all the difference if you know someone is going through the grief and trauma of pregnancy loss, or any loss or grief for that matter: asking them how they are really is a way to connect with them during what can be the most isolating time of their life.

'There is a stigma around asking a grieving person how they are,' explains the Mindful Grief Coach Tahnee Knowles. 'As a bereaved mother, I know that most of the time when people asked me that, they were just being polite. If I was to reveal to them how I'm REALLY doing, they would run a mile. It would be far too heavy for them. So, like many other grievers, I simply say, "OK, thanks, you?"'

Her advice is as follows: 'If you're open to actually listening and care about what my real response is, then ask me this instead: "How are you... really?" This gives me the space to share, and it lets me know that you have the capacity to listen. It's a signal to say that while you may not "get it" you are willing to open your heart with compassion to how it may feel to live through such a devastating time.'

When we experience baby loss, we experience the shattering of our dreams, our plans for the future, which we have been forming since childhood. And on top of all that, we can experience a more subtle loss too. A loss that often those outside the baby-loss community are oblivious to – we lose our identity and our ability to trust a world we think we know so well. We lose confidence in our bodies, our community status, our abilities, our womanhood. Our grasp on reality alters, as does our perception of both our own lives and the lives of others around us. Our whole world changes in the instant that we discover that our baby will not make it into our arms. This isn't dramatic or attention seeking – this is truth.

So, how are you, really? Try it, not just the next time you are meeting someone who is grieving, but with anyone and everyone. You would be surprised how often people answer automatically, but this simple suggestion that you care about hearing more connects us more deeply and honestly.

FINDING YOUR OWN WAY

It's all very well and good us being Little Miss Bossy Pants and telling you different ways of dealing with your loss, but ultimately it is completely and utterly down to you. What feels right *for you* is something only you can answer. And whatever that may be, whatever route you go down, is blimmin' wonderful if you get even an ounce of comfort from it. Hannah's and Chris's stories are powerful examples of just how important this is, and of how the isolation of baby loss can affect your relationships with others.

*

Hannah Foster had no choices left when she had a molar pregnancy (see page 264): trying again wasn't an option for her. And so she had to reframe her situation and find an alternative focus. Having that focus was key – be it exercise or crochet or knitting, anything that occupies and engages your mind is a remedy.

HANNAH'S STORY

'The goal is to just get out, to get fresh air, to see other humans – even if you don't talk to anybody.'

At my twelve-week scan I found out I had no baby. I had what was called a molar pregnancy and I felt so angry and betrayed by my body because it hadn't done what it was supposed to have done. I couldn't even say I'd had a miscarriage because there was no baby at all, just cells.

The odds of having a molar pregnancy are one in 600 and I just felt so isolated. I didn't feel that I fitted in with others who had a miscarriage because this was so different. It was exhausting explaining to everyone what had happened, so in the end I said I had suffered a complicated miscarriage. But the problem with a molar pregnancy is that you can't compare it with a miscarriage because the recovery is so different. With a complete molar pregnancy there are further complications, and in 14 per cent of cases a complete mole [the mass of cells that forms instead of the embryo] can become cancerous. So on top of the anger I felt that my body had let me down, I was gripped with fear too – did I have cancer?

You can't even think about trying to conceive again because you must be constantly monitored and tested, and because it was discovered that I did have cancer, I had to have chemo. A molar pregnancy is so complicated to talk about and for people to understand, it is easy to shut yourself away and hide from the world. I felt so lonely during that time. I didn't think there was anyone who understood what I was going through and when I went on social media, I think I found two or maybe three posts on Instagram from women who'd had MPs.

I remember one of my friends said they hadn't got the mental capacity to take on anybody else's trauma or drama, and I felt like saying, 'Well, that's great, but where does that leave me?! I need to interact and talk to people, and this is the biggest thing in my life right now, so effectively you are forcing me to isolate.' It's not like I wanted to talk about it all the time either. I didn't want it to be the only subject of conversation, but if I was asked how I was, I wanted to say, 'I feel like shit,' and not pussy-foot around people!

So it was a vicious circle – it was easier for me not to see people and to sit at home and wallow and be isolated, to hide, to shut myself away. But – I really want to say this – please, don't do that! Please go out. Just go out. It doesn't matter what day it is, what time it is; don't lock yourself away. It doesn't always matter if the person you see or speak to knows what's going on either; the goal is just to get out of the house, to get fresh air, to see other humans.

I also started a journal, and I spent a lot of time doodling, writing and blogging. It was easier to be honest on paper rather than face to face. And then, when I felt ready, I could share my writing and I didn't have to explain everything again. If friends or family asked me how I felt on a particular day and I would reply, 'Actually, I feel really shit because of that…' they knew what 'that' was. Exercise also helped me a lot. I worked out all the way through my treatment, all the way through the whole shebang, because it gave me an hour, two or three times a week, to forget.

Hannah Foster (S1, E8)

Chris Binnie found that during the process of coming to terms with baby loss he re-evaluated everything – from his friendships to what really matters in life. If you've only picked up this chapter and want to know more of Chris's story, the first part is in Chapter 1: Dealing with Grief, page 23.

CHRIS'S STORY, PART TWO

'Bereaved parents realign who we think is important in life. You can sometimes end up cutting people out because you no longer suffer fools the way you used to.'

After Henry died, we heard all sorts of things from lots of different people, and I have wrestled with some of the platitudes that people throw out for many years. I have reached the conclusion that because we are so bad societally at talking about death, people don't know what to say. I used to rage about that, but now I rationalise it. I rationalise it on the basis that people recognise baby loss as the worst thing that can happen to other people, but because it hasn't happened to them, their only reference point is the worst thing that has ever happened to them.

I am going to use a facile example, which is, if the worst thing that has ever happened to you is that you stubbed your toe once and it hurt like hell, this is the benchmark. Obviously, this is a deliberately ridiculous example, but if you have never lost anybody and you have never been through anything remotely traumatic, then your stubbed toe is your only reference point.

But ideally, of course, you would have sufficient self-awareness to think that in your head but never say it out loud. Empathy and self-awareness aren't mutually inclusive, of course.

I do understand why people struggle with what to say. Some people don't say anything and leave you alone. My friend, who had a toddler called Henry, vanished completely. I never truly understood her reasons – we had been friends for years. But the problem is, the longer friends remain silent, the longer they leave it, the harder it is to row back from that.

Bereaved parents realign who and what we think is important in life very quickly, because our whole perspective on what matters has changed entirely. And so, if you aren't there, if you disappear without a trace, we might give you a few weeks' grace, but when we really needed you, where were you? And while you might have been my best friend for the past fifteen years, when the chips were down and I needed you, where were you then? So therefore, I survived without you. I don't need you anymore. And like many other bereaved parents, you can sometimes just end up cutting people out.

Simultaneously you become more empathetic. Small stuff doesn't matter to you anymore – I don't care about the guy who got that parking space ahead of me, or the woman who cut in front of me for the last supermarket trolley – none of that matters anymore. I don't care. Have my car-parking space, have my trolley... nobody died. It realigns how you think about how the world works and how your world works.

Chris Binnie (S2, E11 and 12)

Chapter 5

Family
Relationships

'The ones who notice the storms in your eyes, the silence in your voice and the heaviness in your heart are the ones who will bring comfort.'

STEVE MARABOLI, AUTHOR

RELATIONSHIP REALITY CHECK

The idea that we are going through our experience of baby loss alone is perhaps true in a physical sense, but equally, in most cases, this is something that two people have come together to dream of and create. And when that dream shatters, two – if not more – hearts are broken, although how you feel will be very different to the feelings of those you hold closest. Your partner isn't going to mirror your grief, and, in turn, you shouldn't try to fit your grief into a shape that suits anyone else. If you can get your head into that space – recognising that we all see and feel things differently – you're heading towards a destination of acceptance and peace.

We naturally judge others by our own standards, which have been created through our own upbringings, experiences and beliefs. These tools we use to create our opinions and judgements will *never* be the same as someone else's.

For example, after a loss, one half of the couple might immediately phone and tell their parents; they may want them to come over to offer support and love. The other half of the couple might decide against telling his/her parents and prefer instead to turn towards their partner for support and to shut out the rest of the world, at least to begin with. The same experience; two different people. A decision affected by how they see the world through a lens created during the course of their life to date.

'Couples can become immune to hearing each other, while voicing their own unmet needs and disappointments,' explains relationship counsellor Lilliana Gibbs. 'And so, they lose contact with each other and the confidence in their capacity to resolve differences. Becoming better equipped to listen, express oneself and work together may require new skills, and being better able to manage one's own emotions. Life is a journey of discovery, with the purpose of becoming more our true selves: to love and be loved and to use our talents to satisfy our needs and pursue our dreams. For this we need to keep growing our self-awareness and stretching our potential, and this is about relationships: our connection to ourselves, the relationship with our partner, and our relations with others.'

Lilliana is pretty nifty when it comes to working with couples during times of grief. We are no experts on this, but it's interesting to hear her take on what couples can do to help support one another, why it's OK to grieve in different ways and why communication is a winner when it comes to problem-solving (it's obvious, really, but sometimes we all need a gentle reminder, so here is yours). Lilliana, over to you…

RELATIONSHIPS IN FOCUS: ME AND YOU – ADVICE FROM LILLIANA GIBBS

Everything I'm talking about here relates to your relationship. To you, the couple; you, the parents. Sudden death knocks us hard – it's disorienting, and the loss of an unborn child is uniquely painful. It's a life that hasn't yet begun… a promise cut short.

Your relationship *will* be impacted. You won't be the same people you were before this event. But I want you to know that working through sadness, giving space for anger and offering support when scared will also connect you. You'll strengthen your bond and know it's safe to tell your partner what you *need,* even if it's something they don't want to hear and can't fix.

Children are conceived in a myriad of constellations: in and out of marriage, to single women, to same-sex couples and to people choosing to co-parent, so it's important to focus on your own relationship, no one else's.

We all need to be seen and heard – it's how we learn and grow. Our need to be witnessed is an important part of the journey. When couples can do this for each other, it's powerfully healing. And when family and friends hold them close, love and comfort are a potent medicine.

THE EFFECTS OF INVISIBLE GRIEF

The intensity of love that parents feel for their baby is not measurable in the weeks or months of pregnancy. Miscarriage can be a strange *invisible grief;* it's not openly talked about or recognised for bereavement leave. Perhaps your pregnancy didn't show yet, or you hadn't shared the news. Most often there's no funeral or ceremony. It can be a lonely loss and this loss can overwhelm relationships. It may also be the first time you are grieving, so you're learning about yourself and each other at the same time.

Grieving differently makes it easy to turn away rather than towards each other. Your partner may be helpless to make the pain go away and so will avoid talking, when there are things that need to be said. Some people isolate themselves to work through their feelings. Others need to talk – they need to share and they need to be heard – while others like to keep their minds busy. And some get too focused on those what-ifs and if-onlys that lead to guilt and fear. For example:

Did I do something to cause this?
If only I was younger…
Why isn't my partner devastated like me?
Will he still want me if I can't have a child?

A woman's sense of identity can be knocked; her new role and her richly imagined future has evaporated along with her baby. The couple can lose their identity as a unit because their future has now been altered. How we navigate this terrain will be influenced by our personality, life experience and circumstances – and, importantly, by the stability of the relationship.

MEN VERSUS WOMEN: HOW WE GRIEVE

It's always good to remember that you and your partner *are* different. How you calm yourselves, how you reflect on and process something that has happened, will vary. And some of these strategies are a lot more effective than others, so it's best to accept that all sorts of feelings may show up. Being allowed to cry, shout, swear, wail or quietly release deep emotions may feel like a roller coaster, but that's all part of being human.

Often men don't get much attention; a baby loss isn't a common topic at work or in the pub. And even those close to him may never ask him how *he's* feeling. For some men it's going to be hard admitting compassion fatigue, and some partners are desperate to fix whatever they can and get 'back to normal'. Some may be afraid to try for another baby; others see no reason to wait.

Women can be upset when their partner isn't as devastated as them, but it's very important to accept the following:

- They may not feel devastated.
- They might not grieve in the same way as you.
- If this is your first pregnancy and your partner already has children, the loss will be more significant to you.
- While your partner's experience may not be as intense, they can still share your suffering because they may also feel very deeply without showing it, particularly if they are a man.
- Be wary of judging their reaction because people travel at different speeds – so this can mean a mismatch in emotional states at any one time.
- Sometimes two people feel much the same emotion, but just express and process it in ways that are hard for their partner to recognise. You then risk disconnecting.

RELATIONSHIP RESILIENCE

The resilience of the relationship depends a lot on the emotional intelligence of both people. By that I mean the capacity to remain present when you are triggered. To self-soothe, reflect, take responsibility for yourself and communicate what's important: all the stuff that is difficult to do when hurting. When you go through something traumatic and personal, like any kind of miscarriage or baby loss, and you go through it together, there is a very good chance of coming out stronger. You may see new aspects in each other and a deeper understanding of the small and big things that bring comfort to each other.

BEREAVED DADS

Experiencing miscarriage or baby loss as a partner is horrendous and very often they are overlooked, with the attention usually focused on the woman who is physically experiencing the loss. And that reinforces the mindset that partners shouldn't seek comfort or that it's 'selfish' if they ask for support. But the emotional side of baby loss is experienced by both parents. The third part of Chris's story (see pages 39 and 120 for Parts One and Two) illustrates this perfectly.

CHRIS'S STORY, PART THREE

'We have a weird triangle image when it comes to grief – Mum is grieving the loss of the baby and Dad's role is to support Mum while she grieves for the loss of her baby.'

I spent most of Thursday, after we found out Wednesday morning that Henry had died, in the garden, with the warm spring sunshine on my face, making phone calls. We had to make sure we told the people we needed to tell, and I didn't want my wife to hear that same conversation over and over again. So even in that moment, before Henry had even been born, I had fallen into that stereotype of what society tells us the role of the male is – which is to take all the responsibility and handle all the stuff for the woman that is grieving. We have this weird triangle image when it comes to grief – Mum is grieving the loss of the baby and Dad's role is to support Mum while she grieves for the loss of her baby. But nobody joins up the other side of the triangle, which is actually that Dad is grieving for the loss of the baby as well.

Over the years, bereaved dads have kicked the door of that misconception down – that the role of the father is not just to support the mother whose baby has died. As a society we have now made an allowance for the fact that Dad is going to grieve for the loss of his baby as well. But we are so indoctrinated to think that men aren't allowed to show emotion in anything or have feelings, and that men talking about their feelings is a sign of weakness, that we internalise it. It's a really damaging misconception about grief full stop, but especially in this context.

I think that is one of the main reasons why there is such a high attrition rate in terms of relationships, because men don't have that outlet to grieve effectively. And sweeping men's grief under the carpet reinforces the message that we shouldn't talk about our feelings. And that is really dangerous.

My outlet for my grief was that I threw myself back into work and used it as a bit of a distraction technique. It doesn't work in the long term, but in the short term it does. I was working in medical sales, so I would spend most of my days in operating theatres, supporting surgeons as they performed surgery. What I found was that, because of the nature of that job, as soon as I went into that operating theatre, I had to concentrate on what was going on in front of me, 100 per cent. Because if I didn't, the surgeons would use the wrong instrument or something catastrophic would happen. I couldn't be distracted by my grief, by my emotional 'baggage'. That couldn't come into the operating theatre with me – although I knew it would be in the changing room waiting for me afterwards. So for, let's say, that three-hour operation (or however long they lasted), I had to park it. I had no choice.

I referee rugby as a hobby too and the same principle applied there. For an hour and a half every Saturday afternoon, if I wasn't concentrating completely on what was going on in front of me, somebody was going to get hurt. So for a small window of time I had to not think about it, and I found that quite a useful process; it gave me a break from my grief on a daily basis. Like most bereaved parents, I have discovered that it is impossible to grieve full-on seven days a week, twenty-four hours a day. You can't do it. You have to find ways to be gentle and let the world back in. The world will carry on. You have to find a way of learning how to adapt to that new normal and what that new normal looks like for you. It takes time to work out. It's a constantly evolving thing because you don't go through a set period of time and everything is OK again, or a set number of 'grieving stages' and you are fixed, it doesn't work like that.

Chris Binnie (S2, E11 and 12)

'This is the saddest place I could ever imagine…'

EXERCISES TO TRY

Lilliana Gibbs has loads of little exercises below that you might want to try if you are part of a grieving couple. Check out her Wobble Theory, too, on page 137 – it's a gem.

THE CONNECTOR EXERCISE

What are the things you can do to best support yourselves through this time? Stay connected through **talk** and **touch.** Grieving and healing is a dual process and is nourished by loving care and time, so here's a lovely little connector exercise. With your partner, take it in turns, one asking the other the three questions, then swapping over.

1. What is something we agree on?
2. What is something you appreciate about me?
3. What is something you'd like me to know?

You don't have to give prolonged or deep and meaningful answers; respond with something that springs to mind. So something you could agree on could be anything from *Game of Thrones* to pistachio ice cream or that you both really wanted your baby.

Respond to each of the answers with a 'thank you'. This is like a little verbal handshake. And remember, this isn't a conversation or a debate. When those three questions are answered, swap over and let your partner tell you their answers.

It's quick, connecting and reminds you both of what you value in the other, while also expressing things that can be empowering.

THE TALKING EXERCISE

Talking enables us to attune to each other, and a rich conversational habit supports and strengthens a relationship. It 'expands' each person and makes it easy to attune to each other. Talking, for some, might sound too much or too uncomfortable… Your partner might think, 'How much talking about this can we keep doing?' But it's necessary to keep an open channel where you can share thoughts and feelings and memories. Talking about what happened and what it means, and what each one needs, allows you to share your dreams and fears too.

This is not a conversation exercise, but two monologues. This is about reflective listening, where partners take it in turns to share their feelings, thoughts, experience, fears… basically whatever they want to express. And the other person just has to listen.

The process does several things: it enables each person to *feel* heard;

it *slows things down*; we can talk and explore a topic without defending our position, and this can bring up new insights. By defining our role as either the **sender** or **receiver**, we *pay attention to just one thing*. Or rather, we just have one job – to either speak or listen. And if we listen, we don't react or think about what we want to say in return.

1. Sit comfortably or lie down. Some couples may be more comfortable gazing at the ceiling rather than making eye contact.
2. For ten minutes, one of you will speak and the other one will listen.
3. From time to time the speaker might want to pause for the listener to reflect back on what they've heard. They don't editorialise; instead, they capture the salient points and feelings.
4. The speaker will naturally clarify anything that has been misheard.
5. Then the couple swap over so the other one speaks for ten minutes.

This is a lovely chance to share yourselves, to be heard without comment or judgment, to listen without needing to fix or change things. Just be heard as you are right now.

THE FIVE-MINUTE CHECK-IN EXERCISE

I often suggest that couples do what I call the five-minute check-in, which is a good daily practice. Over a morning brew, one tells the other how they feel, how they slept, something they thought of or dreamed of or are anxious about… It's like a daily temperature check, which can be really useful for keeping you both attuned to each other.

THE FOUR-STEP EXERCISE

When there is a whiff of conflict, try using this very simple, effective little dispute-resolving tool. It won't work if you're angry or upset, because we tend to fall into negative patterns of communication then. Learn to talk well and discuss how you are specifically offering affection rather than judgement, put-downs or blame.

The four-step process works to rapidly resolve relationship glitches by cutting to the chase, acknowledging the emotive/blaming bits without being derailed by them and suggesting the all-important *repair* element.

Here's how it works. When one partner has an issue with the other, they should express it clearly in these four sentences:

1. This is what I experienced.
2. This is the story I told myself.
3. This is how I felt.
4. This is what I'd like now.

Here's an example, to show the technique in action:

1. **This is what I experienced.** In other words, describe the facts.
   I was expecting you back by seven, but you arrived half an hour late and didn't call me.

2. **This is the story I told myself.** This is the emotion, meaning and conclusion we patch together into a narrative we tell ourselves. It's your STORY.
   You put more value on your own time than mine. You don't care if I'm waiting for you because you have more important things to do.

3. **This is how I felt.** Keep this short, just name your feelings.
   Furious, frustrated, sad and neglected.

4. **This is what I'd like now.** What can be done to fix things, to compensate, to apologise, to understand each other? Keep things simple.
   I'd like to know you heard me, and for you to acknowledge my feelings.

Once we remove the criticism, judgement and defence, we are much more able to listen **and** to be heard. Keep it short, keep it clean.

Often this will be a two-way process, so take turns expressing sentences 1, 2 and 3. Then, when you've both heard each other and feel you can move on to repair, share your number 4s. *What I'd like now is…*

AND WHAT ABOUT TOUCH?

Touch means a lot of things and is often our deepest security. For some, touch and physical affection means loving reassurance. Often it can be good to **touch** and *not to* **talk.** Hugging is powerful, restorative and comforting. Hugging feels good, and you don't have to *feel* like hugging to do it anyway. Because once you hug, you'll enjoy it. Hugging can make you happy anytime/anywhere.

If you're already big huggers, try doing it for much longer – stay a while in a comfortable, relaxing hug. When your hearts are touching, your breathing may naturally attune.

THE WOBBLE THEORY

In every relationship there are going to be upsets or ruptures – that's life. Some of this is unavoidable but, rather than focus on the rupture, it's the repair bit that's so important. Working through and resolving the stuff that threatens your connection is key, and the good news is that it's *because* of all the push and pull and working stuff out that we grow relationship resilience.

All of us have wobbles from time to time: stress, fear, loss of confidence, hurt feelings – whatever it is, we will wobble. We're triggered, we lose our balance, we dysregulate. When one is off-balance it affects the partner, and they may then start to wobble too – this is never good. Arguments thrive in this ecosystem.

When you learn to tolerate your partner's wobble, they can then regulate from you and settle down faster. When your partner sees your distress and remains a steady presence, soon you will become calm and reassured. It works both ways! So each knows that if the other has a wobble, they themselves can be that solid and calm partner.

'One of the sincerest forms of respect is actually listening to what another has to say.'

FACING LOSS AS A COUPLE

One day Bex messaged me (Laura) to say she had been listening to a cool podcast called *Heavy Mental* and suggested we get the couple who host it on our show. I was already organising for them to be on our podcast because I had thought the exact same thing – great minds! Rhys and Leila King are a beautiful couple, who are very self-aware and able to articulate their feelings to each other. Plus, we love a Welsh accent. And they had a fancy mic, which really showed us up!

LEILA AND RHYS'S STORY

*'We have dealt with healing differently and that can be hard,
because you want someone to heal the same way as you so
you can understand that they are in as much pain as you.'*

Leila: Not long after getting together I accidently got pregnant, which was a bit of a shock. At our twelve-week scan, we were told that the baby had died at seven weeks but I hadn't had a miscarriage, and that was just the beginning of the absolute shitshow that is our attempt to have a baby. It was extremely traumatic for a new couple to be going through this; we were still figuring out how to be in a new relationship and then thinking that we were going to have a baby together but then being told we weren't. I had the added trauma of carrying the baby for about three weeks after finding out it had died, because they had to keep scanning me to check I hadn't got my dates wrong.

I chose to do the induction of the miscarriage at home, but we weren't really told how bad it would be or that the baby would be completely intact, so it was a lot to deal with. But we survived as a couple, we got married and six months after that we started trying again and got pregnant straight away. But at our twelve-week scan they told us the baby was alive and kicking but had something called a cystic hygroma, which is a cluster of cells on the back of the neck, and that is what they measure when they check whether the baby has chromosomal abnormalities.

They wanted to carry on with tests if I was happy to carry on with the pregnancy, so from twelve weeks to twenty weeks it was just a horrendous waiting game. I was five months pregnant when we finally got some answers, and the list of things that were going to be wrong with our little boy was just astronomical – but they couldn't give us any definite answers either. He could be blind; he could be deaf; he could be autistic; he could have learning difficulties; he could have a hole in his heart – and then they said he 'could be' all of these things. It was just too much of a gamble and so we decided not to continue with the pregnancy.

Rhys: It was a whole period of uncertainty. Ups and downs of thinking maybe we can do this, but then having difficult discussions around whether it was fair to bring a life into the world who will potentially know a lot more suffering than another child would if they were born completely healthy. The uncertainty was the main driving emotion, because we couldn't have definitive answers.

Leila: When we ended the pregnancy, I didn't appreciate that I would have to give birth to him. It was full-blown labour with midwives in a hospital. We were in a special suite called the Snowdrop suite, which is why we called our son Snow.

I knew I wanted to see him afterwards. I was having counselling at the time and my counsellor said to me, 'Think about whether you want to buy him anything or read him a story,' and at the time I thought, 'That's so sad, I can't even fathom the thought of reading my dead son a story!' But when I was in the moment, that was all I wanted to do – be a mum to him.

We had some photos with him too. It's so bizarre because if someone had said to me we would be having a family photo beforehand, I would have thought that would be too heart-breaking, but I am so glad we have these photos.

Rhys: I was allowed in for the birth, and afterwards it felt so natural to hold Snow, completely normal. I felt so guilty that

Leila had to go through such physical pain, and I just felt helpless, looking on. I just wanted to drastically make things better, but I couldn't, and obviously it was just a completely different experience to Leila's, and that was hard. The ways in which we grieved were different – hers was more traditional; mine tended to go into a very obsessional controlling type of behaviour after the event, as a way of trying to control something because the whole event felt very out of control.

Leila: We have dealt with healing differently and that can be hard, because you want someone to heal the same way as you. But through a lot of communication, we understand that that's OK. We have a stronger understanding of each other, and we are stronger as a couple.

Unfortunately, we have gone on to lose another two babies since Snow – both early losses, but it doesn't take away the pain that it's early because, to us, that is four babies we have lost now. With each one we are getting better at dealing with it – the recovery time seems better each time – and because we know each other so well in these traumatic situations, we know we can get through them.

Rhys and Leila King (S2, E21 and 22)

FAMILY: SHARING IS CARING

There is a lot about baby loss which your wider family won't have a clue about (and likewise, we didn't know about) until it happens. As we've said before, we fully believe that while baby loss cannot be understood at an emotional level unless you have first-hand experience, it can be understood at an educational level – we can teach others how to react to those who have lost, and we owe it to all women to do this. If we can make this awful experience slightly less horrendous for women in the future, then we must.

So let's start with friends and family. Let's make sure they are aware of what happens after baby loss – not just the brutalities of the physical aspect, but the other, more visceral side of things. The deep and the frightening darkness that follows. The confusing, exhausting and heart-breaking headspace we enter into after our experience. Direct them to this page – or shove it directly under their nose. Whatever works in your famalam.

We feel isolated: When we lose our baby, initially we are given sympathy, but as time moves on people expect us to recover. We then feel like we are bringing down the mood of any family occasion with our broken hearts and our inability to 'cheer up'. And then sometimes we stop talking and stop coming to family events. This makes us feel incredibly alone.

We feel shame: We as women have an inbuilt narrative that has existed for decades and dictates that we ought to become mothers. When our baby dies, we often subconsciously feel as though there is something wrong with us and we have failed.

We lose our confidence: When our baby dies we lose faith in our capabilities. We are no longer living out the reality of motherhood that we expected. We realise how little control we have over our physical selves, and as such, we completely lose faith and confidence in the ability of our own body.

We feel lost: Often we grow up with an unrealistic idea of fertility and pregnancy. Our dreams of becoming a mother are rehearsed in role play as children, and when we later see those blue lines as an adult, those dreams become a reality. When our baby dies we come unstuck – we can start to distrust the world that has reinforced this false narrative.

We feel left behind: But we don't necessarily want to move forward either. We can feel isolated and left behind by others when we are still grieving and they have moved on. However, the thought of feeling better is frightening and overwhelming. We worry that it means we will be forgetting our baby, and this breaks our heart.

'If today all you did was hold yourself together, we are proud of you.'

TAKING TIME FOR SIBLINGS

If you have another child or children at home, it's fair to say it won't just be the relationship between you and your partner that will be impacted by pregnancy loss. Explaining the loss of a sibling is likely to be painful and difficult to navigate for you, as well as painful and difficult to understand for another child. Depending on their age, they may have lots of questions, lots of emotional outbursts and lots of worry around what has happened, and so it's important to involve your children in the grieving process and be as open and honest as you can with them.

Equally, it may not seem like your other children care at all. They may take it all in their stride and potter off to do something else. This, too, can be hard to take onboard. Often, when this is the case, children come back with thoughts and questions once they've processed the news. We go into this in more detail in Chapter 9.

See the Resources section at the end of the book (page 275) for some recommended books to help facilitate these conversations with little ones. There is also a podcast episode all about sibling loss which we recorded with Emma Poore, and which you might find useful (S1, E13).

Dealing with sibling loss

When I discovered that our baby had died, my children didn't know that I was pregnant. I wasn't sure whether to tell them; I wanted to save them from the heartache, but I felt that by not telling them I would be denying the existence of a baby that was part of our family. I took my eldest two children for a walk and explained what had happened, and because the miscarriage was missed and the medication I'd taken had not yet worked, I was still carrying our baby. My daughter put her hand on my tummy and said, 'I'm happy that I got to say goodbye, but I'm so sad our baby won't get to see this beautiful world.' She was seven and the comment broke me, but equally, the fact that she immediately recognised the importance of our baby and their place in our family was a huge comfort.

Bex

GRANDPARENT GUILT

When you experience baby loss, alongside your own grief, you can feel a tremendous amount of guilt about what you perceive to be denying others. The pile of shitty feelings continues to grow. Essentially, you blame yourself for not living up to the expectations you had of your role as a daughter or daughter-in-law. You feel you've denied both sets of parents the opportunity and title of 'doting grandparent'. This is often subconscious, but it can weigh so heavily on our shoulders. We can start to become irrational and defensive, particularly around in-laws, worried that we've not 'produced' a child for their son. We feel guilty seeing our parents and knowing they long to be grandparents, all the while feeling that this is something we have 'failed to deliver'.

This is obviously complete madness, but, while we know that this sense of guilt is misplaced, we also feel it to the very core.

The wider family often throw in excruciating one-liners at Christmas and get-togethers. 'Any news?' or 'Do we hear the patter of tiny feet?' are just a couple of phrases that often come out when we're in a long-term relationship or following a wedding. These comments compound our feelings of guilt and all-round shittiness and, as the family members who are in the know avert their gaze, unsure of what to say, it can leave our already broken heart more bruised than we can handle.

> **Guilt, paranoia and isolation**
>
> I struggled with this a lot. It was completely unfounded, but at my lowest I thought a lot about what people must be thinking about my inability to carry a baby. Did my husband want to be with someone else who could give him a baby? Did my in-laws think that their son deserved better? Did my mum feel disappointed in my inability to provide a grandchild? I guess I was just paranoid and full of self-loathing and self-doubt. It's a shitty place to find yourself, not trusting the world around you, even those you are closest to. This really is isolation at its worst!
>
> Laura

GRIEF ACROSS CULTURES

We wanted to talk to Noma Mzenda-Emego after she mentioned to us about the huge cultural differences between her home country of Zimbabwe and the UK which she encountered after her baby loss – particularly in her own family's reaction to the news. This was also one of the first podcasts in which we spoke in detail about the physicality of holding your lost baby, and this incredible woman wanted to share that so other people knew what to expect.

NOMA'S STORY

'In Africa, it's their belief that a mother can't grieve for something they never saw, and that's it. Baby loss is never talked about.'

I was four months pregnant when I suffered horrific back pain at work and went to the toilet, realising something was very wrong. I put my hand between my legs and thought I felt my baby's head, only to be told when I arrived at the hospital later that it was the membrane that had come out and my baby had no heartbeat.

The doctors told me I had an incompetent cervix [see page 261], which is why it just opened up and my son came with no warning at sixteen weeks. They then told me I would have to give birth to my son, and after several hours they induced me and I started getting contractions. I was in complete shock. I had no idea I would have to actually give birth and I had no idea what a 16-week-old baby would look like.

My husband Rod and I are both from Africa; I am from Zimbabwe and he is from central Africa. We had been trying to get pregnant for quite a while and I had suffered two miscarriages and a chemical pregnancy before I fell pregnant with my son in the midst of COVID in May 2020.

After I had given birth, the midwife asked if we wanted to spend time with our son. They had cleaned him up and dressed him. I was terrified and I didn't know if we should hold him. But then my husband looked at me, as if to say, 'It's OK,' and I am glad I had that time with him. Idris was a real baby. I feel like, if I hadn't seen him, I am not sure I would have believed I was pregnant at all. The midwife treated Idris like he was alive, and she brought him back to me 'for cuddles' she said, and I lay him next to me, fixing his blanket and singing to him.

When we left hospital, all I felt was that my body had let me down and I was abandoning my baby. I knew he wasn't alive and it wasn't rational, but what if he wants his mummy? What if he is cold? I felt like I was leaving him with strangers as we walked out of the hospital with just a memory box and no baby.

I was in complete shock, and I cried a lot during that time. I didn't know what to do. In Africa, if you have a miscarriage or stillbirth, they are not treated as a baby. No one talks about it; they dispose of it and you go home. It's their belief that a mother can't grieve for something they never saw and that's it, it's never talked about.

I had just lost a baby and I didn't know what I should do. I remember talking to my mum. I needed to talk to her, as I was so devastated, and my mum, coming from her African point of view, just said, 'I don't know what you should do. I don't know why you had to see it.' We couldn't reach out to any family because it's just not talked about, and that's the hardest bit. When I finally talked to my mum properly about it and she asked me what happened, she just said, 'I didn't realise you had to give birth to him. You need to stop crying, his soul won't go into heaven. There is a reason why it happened.' And that was so hard. I just shut out family members after that. I knew I wouldn't get any sympathy or consolation or understanding, because they just don't deal with it.

My husband's side of the family didn't say anything either.

One of his uncles simply said to him, 'You need to be strong for your wife.' And my husband and I did talk – we talked about our son quite a lot. He was quite open and he would listen, and although he would never start the conversation because he said he didn't want to bring it up in case I got upset, he would always respond if I talked about it. I found him some support groups to reach out to, but he didn't do any of that at the time. Only now is he ready to reach out to other dads. It's interesting for an African man to say that because they are always told they have to be strong and carry on, and not talk about it because that's just the way it is.

Noma Mzenda-Emego (S1, E11)

SPECIAL OCCASIONS – THE SHITSHOW MAGNIFIED

Big family get-togethers, special occasions, birthdays, Christmas… they are a ball-ache (mildly put) and the upshot of going to them means our feelings of trauma and grief are often going to be magnified tenfold. While we know we could sit here and tell you to avoid each and every one of these events, we also know that's not realistic or possible. Instead, we will arm you with an emotional toolbox, full of coping mechanisms and back-up plans. It is also worth saying here that you do not *have* to attend any event if you don't want to. Remember those boundaries. Your needs do not, and should not, come at the bottom of the pile. Give yourself permission to stay at home if you need to.

1. Know your limitations

If the occasion is likely to entail more stress than enjoyment, it might be worth accepting that declining the invite right from the word go is the best option. There is no family occasion that is worth that pain.

You could always try to make a one-on-one plan to celebrate with the host another time instead.

2. Stick to your guns

If you know it's going to be a long event, why not say from the outset that you can only come for a short period of time? If you let the host or family know this ahead of time, there should be no guilt trip when you do leave, but if you do feel pressured into staying when it's all becoming overwhelming, just go. Stick to your guns and head for the door when you feel the need to.

3. Choose your battles

If you face any of the misconceptions, 'at leasts' or totally inconsiderate comments from relatives that we discussed in Chapter 3 (and let's face it, we all have a relative who doesn't have an emotional/social bone in their bodies), you can play it two ways. Leave (good idea) or try to educate them instead (good idea). Be honest with them. Tell them what a shitshow it is. Silence their misconceptions – not to shame them, but to help them understand. Perhaps their glib, hurtful comments won't come so easily in the future. Equally, this is not your fight alone, so if you're not feeling up to it, leave it for another warrior today.

4. Don't feel bad

Sometimes a change of scene or seeing friends who have no idea about what you have gone through can give you a sense of freedom. You don't have to feel that everyone is waiting for you to act in a certain way or judging how you react to things. You can, for an hour or so, take a break. And don't feel bad if for that short, short time you enjoy a drink with a friend, or laugh at Uncle Nigel's horrifically bad jokes (however unlikely this seems). You are allowed to enjoy yourself.

5. You don't owe anyone

Being invited to a big do or a special occasion can instantly trigger a feeling of obligation – you 'must' attend because you have been 'chosen'. The point is, while it's nice to be invited to super-special or intimate occasions (smaller gatherings can be just as hard as larger occasions, as you might feel trapped and unable to slip away quite so easily), you don't owe anyone an explanation if you don't go. Simple. As.

6. Tackle the tunes

Music evokes all sorts of memories and emotions, and these things can't be anticipated or guarded against. A song on the radio can blindside you as you idly do the washing-up just as much as a song played by an out-of-tune band at a family wedding can. Unless you go around with ear defenders on – and we can't think of many outfits they'd complement – there is zero chance of you being able to prevent this from ever happening. But songs don't last forever. Turn the volume down, leave the room or listen to the song, acknowledging the memory and the emotion it brings. Hell, sing along at the top of your lungs if you need to.

7. Go empty-handed

The giving and receiving of gifts is quite frankly the last bloomin' thing that should take up your time and energy in the midst of grief, and yet these are the mundane things that tell us the world keeps on spinning, even though we are screaming silently for it to stop and give us a break. Receiving gifts doesn't make us suddenly happy, as there is nothing we would want unless it's having our baby back. And giving gifts takes thought, time, effort and expense – all things we don't have the headspace for, and don't want to have the headspace for. No one is going to judge you if you go empty-handed. If you decide to go, that will be enough.

8. Your clothes, your choice

Getting out of the house will mean getting out of perhaps the comfort of the clothes that we feel most relaxed in – we won't bother saying 'loungewear' because, let's face it, we mean pyjamas. So when we are invited to social gatherings, the idea of taking off our 'safe' clothes – our comfort blankets, as it were – seems like a monumental ask. Don't think that going out means dressing to the nines. Sure, you might feel that this is an ideal opportunity to go all out (sometimes going the full hog might feel like an appealing change), but equally no one is going to know better than you what to wear. Be seen. Wear colour. Paint your nails. If making an effort seems like a good distraction, go for it.

'On the darkest days, I wear the brightest lipstick.'
CHARLA GRANT, THE GRATEFUL HEARTS CLUB

9. Have a wingwoman

Having someone to generally have your back at any social engagement is going to be a game-changer. If possible, take someone to keep you from standing on your own; to intercept those relatives who are annoying/overly excitable (insert your own annoyances here); to walk outside with you if you need a breather; to hold a conversation in the group if speaking becomes too much; to stage an intervention to prevent you from drinking that final glass of Prosecco. Even if they don't stay stuck like glue to you at all times, having someone there who *knows* you and knows how *to be there* for you is going to give you confidence and security.

*'Even now, as broken as you may feel, you are still so
strong. There is something to be said for how you hold
yourself together and keep moving, even though you
feel like shattering. This is your healing. Don't stop. It
doesn't have to be pretty, you just have to keep going.'*

THE BIGGIES

Christmas

With celebrations around a specific time of year, there will be an
enforced sense of joviality, merriment and holiday fun. Yep, we're
talking about the C-word. At Christmas, it feels as though we are
assaulted by the happiness of others, and perhaps our previous jolly
traditions now feel hollow and empty. Christmas is going to be one of
the hardest times, because it centres on the family and, more specifically,
children. It can remind us of our own empty nest. It can be especially
hard if you have other children because your sense of guilt around
making sure they have a magical time is likely to take all your strength.
We see you, warrior. It also offers up office parties, where Susan from
Accounts uses fertility as small talk. 'So have you got kids?' etc., etc.

The best way to deal with this time of year is to focus on one day
at a time and not become overwhelmed by the whole season. Say
no to Christmas office parties. Plan new Christmas traditions that
mean something to you at this moment in your life. Go somewhere
completely different during the whole shebang and take yourself
away from the family frivolities if you so wish – the point is, you
mustn't feel guilty about things you think you 'should' be doing at
this time of year.

Mother's Day: Not all mothers get to take their babies home

Here at *TWGGE* we know personally just how triggering holidays and special events can be when you've lost a baby, and Mother's Day is no exception – in fact, it's probably the hardest. A day designed around the love that you so desperately crave; the love that morphed into grief when you discovered that your baby wasn't going to be a part of this physical world. Ugly feelings rise (see Chapter 6) and we can feel desperately isolated in our pain, unable to fully comprehend or explain it.

Remember, on Mother's Day (and every other day that you find triggering) there are no hard and fast rules. If you want to celebrate with your own mum, do it. If you'd rather delay that celebration and spend the day with friends, your partner or alone, that's fine too. Silence media posts and turn off the radio if it's churning out 'thanks, Mum' shout-outs.

There is no shame in feeling grotty. Mother's Day isn't as simple as a mum being spoilt by her children. Mother's Day can be challenging for many reasons, not just for those in this community, but for those who are missing someone or those who do not have the relationship they would like with their mum. The truth is, we never know the path that someone else is walking, so it's important to be kind.

'Kindness is free, sprinkle that shit everywhere!'

The challenge of Mother's Day

For six years, I absolutely dreaded Mother's Day. I lost multiple pregnancies in that time and each year, when this celebration came around, it felt like a kick in the teeth. It wasn't the gifts and cards or even the afternoon tea that I wanted; I just longed to have my very own snotty little person who would make me a cup of lukewarm tea and rip daffodils out of the garden *for me – because I was their mummy*. Mother's Day just served as a reminder of my failure to do what seemed to come so easily to others, and I was left wondering if I would ever have a baby.

Laura

So next time you face a big event or family gathering, remember, this too shall pass. A day is just a day. The lead-up is often worse than the actual event, so try to remember that it can be empowering to choose the time to make new memories. Do what's right for you and feel no pressure. We're proud of you.

Chapter 6

Ugly Feelings

'You are not a shit.'

Ugly feelings and validation are two of the most common things we are contacted about in *TWGGE*, which is probably why we bang on about these topics so much – #sorrynotsorry!

Whenever we post about ugly feelings on social media, there is always someone who pipes up to say that they don't struggle with them. They feel nothing but happiness and warmth in the situations that make the rest of us feel like shit, and while that's admirable and totally amazing for them, we know from chatting to others that it is *these* individuals who are in the minority. The majority of us say 'fuck you' under our breath (or out loud) as we scroll through Facebook and see that Dan and Susie are expecting, following a 'whirlwind romance'.

As well as beating ourselves up (see Chapter 3), we might start thinking the vilest thoughts about someone we love when we see them getting the family we want. Your best mate, or your sister even, might be targets.

You start to get consumed by intrusive thoughts: 'Why her and not me?' 'I deserve this more.' 'I've been trying longer,' etc. You might feel differently towards different people in different situations, depending on your own triggers. Your response might be worse when pregnancies occur seemingly 'by accident'. These feelings can lead to shame, self-hatred and a sense that you are completely out of control, that you don't recognise yourself anymore. Who have you become? You can't see a way out of it and you can't *get* out of it, and those ugly thoughts just drive you mad. They are exhausting and depressing.

It's a difficult thing to get your head around. So we want you to remember some important things: just because the first thought that comes into your head is not positive, it does not say anything about you. All it says is that you are in a really shit situation. Ugly feelings suck, but they don't make you an ugly person. They make you a very, very ordinary person… Ugly feelings are a common reaction to a terrible situation.

When you see a pregnancy announcement…

If you feel: *sad, angry, pissed off, livid, jealous, down, distraught, hopeless, unkind, bitter, anxious, muted, spiteful, annoyed, desperate, ragey, unchari-table, low, furious, confused, shocked, heartbroken, sombre, traumatised…*
THAT'S OK. THAT'S NOTHING OUT OF THE ORDINARY.

YOU ARE NOT YOUR FEELINGS

Does this happen when you see a pregnancy announcement?

1. You feel like shit.
2. You feel like shit for feeling like shit.
3. You repeat Steps 1 and 2 for way longer than you would like.

Yes? Congratulations! You're a completely typical *TWGGE* member.

Who can relate to this barrel of laughs? Step on up to the seemingly never-ending cycle of shit.

Someone you like, someone you love even, announces a pregnancy, and even if they do it the right way (they tell you by text rather than blindsiding you with a social media post, and they are kind to you because they recognise that this will be hard for you to hear. They literally tick all those considerate boxes), YOU WILL STILL FEEL LIKE SHIT.

Then comes the really shitty shit. You feel like you are a shitty person; the shittiest of people, because you can't even justify feeling like shit – they did everything right! You can't even wallow in your shitty feelings because you don't feel like you are entitled to them…

'YOU ARE NOT A SHIT'

It's just the way it is. You are not your ugly feelings. You are an amazing, awesome, beautiful mix of beliefs, ideas and dreams. If you try to suppress those shitty feelings, if you dwell on them and allow them to whisper nasty untruths in your ear, they will consume you, and you are not that person.

You have to feel the feelings. If you deny them, they will linger around for longer… It makes them more frightening and gives them more power. They will eat you up inside if you let them, so instead, acknowledge them and accept them. Give the ugly feelings room to breathe and have a run around up there; observe them and then you will be able to manage them.

Talk to someone, message someone, walk with someone. Just don't succumb to the belief that your thoughts make you anything other than human, because they really, really don't.

Take it from us, you are pretty bloody awesome.

UGLY FEELING #1: ANGER

A red-hot emotion, this bugger. It's one of the biggies. Alongside jealousy (see ugly feeling #3, below), anger can simmer away for days/weeks/months or erupt in a cacophony of swearing, sweat and tears.

And it takes many guises: *It's not fair; I hate myself; No one cares; Everyone has moved on and forgotten that I am in turmoil; No one sees my pain; No one asks me about my pain; No one wants to know; Why isn't my partner as upset as me? I don't want to go out; I don't want to see anyone; I hate pregnant women; Why do other women have it so easy? She doesn't deserve to be pregnant, she is not as nice as me; My body has let me down; All I wanted was a baby, why is that so hard? Why can't my body function as it should?*

'Can you relate to any of the above? Often these angry thoughts are the ones that haunt us afterwards. We feel hot with rage, which often gives way to feelings of shame or embarrassment because we don't like this angry person we have become.

Well, we're here to let you know that anger is a very, very common emotion. It's part of the grieving process and is definitely not ABNORMAL.

Sometimes you might find yourself totally consumed by anger for no apparent reason. You might fly into a rage in the supermarket because they have sold out of four-pinter milks and instead you have to buy double the number of two-pinters, which is NOT WHAT YOU F**KING WELL WANTED.

You might find that WhatsApp chats, books, Facebook or leftover ovulation and pregnancy tests trigger the rage. So, what can you do?

Mute the chats. Leave Facebook. Step away from the dairy section in the supermarket. Play loud music, take a golf club to a bush in the garden, punch a cushion, run, go for a ragey power walk, write everything down that is in your head – even if it doesn't make sense. Scream. Take crockery you don't want anymore and throw it against a wall.[1]

Trust us. It will help. We have found that if you can create an outlet for this angry energy, you can channel it and it will subside faster. Even talking about your ugly anger will help you feel better. Recognising it is half the battle, so don't be scared of it.

'Anger is not who you are, it's how you are feeling. It's normal.'

UGLY FEELING #2: ENVY

Envy is such a painful feeling. You may feel envious of the couple who 'weren't even trying'; the couple who 'didn't want a baby yet but... oops!'; couples who have just got together; friends who started trying to get pregnant way after you. Then there are the posts on social media, joking about how easy it was. Women who moan about how difficult parenting is – how they're not getting any sleep, how toddlers are a nightmare. You might find it difficult to hear about women who fall pregnant after casual sex, or those who haven't given up drinking, don't take supplements, haven't experienced the obsession and trauma of trying again after loss.

UGLY FEELING #3: JEALOUSY

WHY HER AND NOT ME? This ring a few ding-a-lings? We don't want to feel this way and we could never admit it – who are we to judge any given person's situation? And yet, the green-eyed monster is a shit of an emotion and will often leave you feeling like the Worst.

---

1 Make sure the wall isn't plasterboard... speaking from experience.

Person. Ever. Especially when the object of your emotions is someone that you know very well, or who is a good friends or relative.

Being very intimately acquainted with the pain that comes with not being able to get pregnant or the heartache of baby loss means you wouldn't wish it upon anyone. Of course, you don't want to take away the happiness Emily, Emma or Evie has (don't ask us why we've gone with these names), but you just don't understand why it's not you. It's like you are standing still while the happy world passes you by because when you have an intense desire for something, coupled with the inability to fulfil that desire, all you are left with is a painful feeling of jealousy. Pregnancy and baby adverts on platforms like Instagram can also trigger those ugly feelings - even when you know they're just marketing. See page 277 in our Resources chapter for some help shutting them up.

We've come to realise that jealousy is a bit like a hangover. When you are in the midst of it, you want to curl up and hide. Time stretches before you like an endless dark void and you just want to feel better, but there is no end in sight. Yet despite the intensity of your suffering, no one 'gets' it. No one co-signs your jealously. But of course, jealousy is not unique to this situation. Everyone has suffered it or will suffer it or is suffering it. And bouts of jealousy, like hangovers, are temporary, so ride this bugger out.

Infertility and loss are so bloody hard to go through; they deplete your energy and your ability to be rational – and that's what's going on here. Jealousy is also an emotion that is completely unavoidable because our fight-or-flight survival brains have felt the feels before our rational brain can stop us and we are sometimes left shocked by the ferocity and darkness of our primitive thoughts.

So yes, confront the jealousy. It does suck, it's going to suck, there is nothing you can do about it. Happy for you, sad for me. Sort of. Being jealous has never felt so ugly. And yet, if we put too much time and energy into other people's business, where does that leave us? If we are so invested in other people's lives and lifestyles and happiness, when do we get time to sort out our own? Push yourself towards your own version of happiness and don't give two figs about anyone else. Sending love.

UGLY FEELING #4: PARANOIA

Jealousy and envy go together with a sprinkle of paranoia, because alongside the hurt and upset that blindsides you when you hear a pregnancy announcement, there is an underlying feeling of paranoia too. You may feel paranoid that other people are hiding their pregnancies from you or that they may get pregnant before you. You distance yourself in an attempt to avoid those situations and to protect yourself from upset. You can feel paranoid that others are questioning how you will 'take' the news.

When ugly feelings strike

I always struggled with the paranoia surrounding other people's happy news. I remember sitting in a church watching our close friends get married and thinking, 'I bet they have a baby before us.' At that point we'd already been trying for five years and had experienced five losses. I felt like we *deserved* to have a baby before them, and I couldn't bear the thought of them beating us to it. I avoided them for about six months, knowing that their 'happy news' would be just around the corner. I hated myself for this. Another issue I had when faced with the news of anyone being pregnant was that the jealousy made me a crazy mad woman, and I didn't know how to deal with it. It didn't matter if it was someone I loved, a colleague, an old school friend, a random stranger or a friend of a friend on social media: the jealousy got me every time. I had no idea how to act in these situations and was paranoid about coming across as bitter and twisted, so I tried to put on a game face. It took everything in me not to run away and cry. I tried to react normally and gracefully, but in my attempt to fake some happiness, I would end up with some over-the-top, squeally, jazz-hands response and feel like a complete plum afterwards, paranoid that everyone could see through it.

Laura

DEALING WITH THE UGLY

U-G-L-Y, you ain't got no alibi...

We need to pull our big-girl pants up in order to deal with these feelings. How? Read on, dear friends, read on...

Don't get caught up: Denying ugly feelings their place makes them more frightening and gives them more power in your mind. You have to have feelings! And if you deny these feelings the little buggers will linger around longer. It's like if someone said to you, 'Don't think about an elephant.' What happens? You can't help but think about a huge grey hunk of an elephant elephanting around. When these ugly feelings appear, allow yourself to remember that you are NORMAL and simply acknowledge them. Let them potter around for a bit and then think about something else.

Tell people what you need: Being told face to face about a baby announcement is possibly the worst situation to be in and it's unlikely you will have any sort of ability to keep your shit together when it happens. In our experience, asking family and friends to share any baby news by text is the best way forward. You can read it, deal with the ugly emotions that come from reading it and then – in time and when you are ready – you can respond. Don't be fooled into thinking you are making their pregnancy news all about you – don't add that guilt to the mix! You're not, you are simply protecting yourself.

Take a step back: Take a step back from a situation that triggers the ugly. You don't have to respond to anything immediately. It's 100 per cent OK to protect yourself and your emotions. In fact, it's not just OK, it is absolutely bloody necessary. Sometimes we need to withdraw slightly to create some space between ourselves and the people or situations that can trigger our ugly feelings. In order to maintain good mental health, it's important to have boundaries in place. We've said it before and we'll say it again: mute the WhatsApp group, decline the baby shower invite, unfollow pregnant friends on socials. And remember, these are your friends; they will understand.

Go with the gut reactions: Scream, shout, cry, howl, rant, nap. Physically you need to let your body react to how it feels, so just go with it. Run, walk, cycle, swim, skip or jump. You might not feel like it, but sometimes having a physical outlet for those ugly thoughts burns them away as you burn the energy. They won't disappear completely, but you can have a breather from them for a while.

Get outside: There is nothing, we repeat *nothing*, more powerful than a bit of fresh air. It can totally change your mood. It won't *always* work, but it's worth trying when you feel the ugliness engulf you. Take a deep breath, go outside and find a patch of grass. Stretch if you want. Close your eyes if you want. Take off your shoes and socks, and feel the grass between your toes; feel the energy in grounding yourself. Go for a walk on a blustery day and feel the wind engulf you and then blow away the ugly thoughts within you. Visualise them leaving you and being lost forever in the wilderness. Face the sun and feel its warmth on your cheeks. There is a reason for the cliché that Mother Nature is so bloody wonderful.

Create: Write, scribble, draw, doodle: let your mind wander in a sub-conscious way so that the pen doesn't leave the paper and you just write without thinking. (Take a look at our journal prompts in Chapter 2 for ideas on how to get started, on page 58). Equally, painting, drawing or colouring are great ways of switching off from the outside world.

Express: Give the feelings airtime, and they will disappear faster. If you try to squash them and spend ages beating yourself up about them, they will get bigger and overwhelm your mind. Have a bloody good moan and rant. These are not shameful feelings, they are normal.

Find your people (we're here for you): Sharing ugly feelings with those who haven't experienced baby loss can be challenging and, ultimately, if they don't understand, can make you feel worse. The baby-loss com-munity is huge and so kind and supportive – we are your people. Please use us. It's so bloody liberating to share how seeing a pregnant lady at the fruit and veg section in Tesco made you want to lob a grapefruit at her. Or how you saw red when you saw Carol announce her pregnancy on Facebook by saying, 'Much to Steve's annoyance we got pregnant the first month of trying. Lol!' LOL, Carol, LO-f**king-L.

Meditate

This word is often bandied about when it comes to mindfulness techniques (have you conjured up images of sitting in complete silence, burning incense or listening to whale music to meditate? Rest assured, that's not what it's all about!). The beauty of meditation really does lie in its simplicity: the act of saying to yourself, 'Right here, right now, I am caring for myself.' This means it is no longer an abstract exercise but something very real.

Set a time limit: If this is new to you, it can help if you set yourself a short period of time to aim for. Five or ten minutes to begin with is plenty.

Take a seat: Choose somewhere quiet and comfy – a place you won't be disturbed or distracted.

Notice your body: Are you able to stay in this position? Are you on a hard floor or sitting on a relaxing chair? If you are able to stay in this position for a while, go with whatever works for you.

Inhale and exhale: Follow the sensation of breathing. Try not to let your mind wander and focus on the breath as it goes in and out of your body. (Of course your mind *will* wander, it's inevitable; just try to bring it back to your breathing when you can.)

Be kind: Don't get cross with yourself if your mind wanders too much and try not to obsess over the contents of your thoughts. Always bring yourself back to your breathing. When you are ready to finish, open your eyes and take in the moment and your surroundings. And pat yourself on the back too. If you can practise this short exercise when you are overwhelmed or overanxious, it will help steady your ship. Good work.

OUR FEELINGS ARE NOT MUTUALLY EXCLUSIVE

We have broken down the most common ugly feelings, but it's worth reminding ourselves that while one of these emotions might be overriding the others, we humans are complex things of beauty, and we have the ability to experience a number of emotions at any given moment.

When we experience baby loss, our overriding feeling is one of sadness, but that doesn't mean we can't experience happiness soon afterwards, even if it's in short measures. These brief instances can make us feel guilty and ashamed because we don't want them there; they make us feel disloyal to our lost baby.

Equally when we get the ugly feelings – the anger, the jealousy, the hatred – alongside feelings of happiness, the uglies are so powerful that they drown out the other emotions and become the focus of our attention.

Feelings aren't mutually exclusive, and we shouldn't think of them as such. No *one* person is all about *one* emotion at any *one* time, and when we can recognise that, we can start to examine our inner selves and let go of feeling shitty, because we know that even our feelings are not alone. It's a big lesson to learn, we know. We've got you.

Chapter 7

Reconnecting with Yourself

'We deny ourselves the space to grieve because we don't feel entitled to the pain.'

We're going on a bit of a rant now, so hold on tight! What has always really pissed us off is that, when we have a miscarriage, we look to the one thing we think failed us – our body – which in turn derails our whole sense of self. Essentially, what we are doing is pinning our worth on just a few organs over which we have no control. Many of us believe that we have been put on this earth to procreate, so when we 'fail' to do that, we wrongly blame ourselves, despite the fact that we have no control over the situation. We forget all the things we once liked about our body and instead become obsessed with what we perceive to be its failures.

Through our own personal experiences, we recognise that the healing process is a holistic one, involving the whole person. Following the loss of a baby, it's easy to distrust your body and this can morph into self-loathing. Your mind and mental health play a crucial role in those emotions. In life, when we are at our best, it's because our mind and body are singing off the same hymn sheet, so getting our mind and body to work in sync is vital. We hope you find this chapter, which focuses on reframing thoughts and physical reconnection, helpful.

'The relationship we have with ourselves is the most important one we can cultivate.'

LOUISA MACINNES, SEX AND RELATIONSHIP COACH

RECONNECTING WITH YOURSELF MENTALLY AND EMOTIONALLY

Mindfulness is a word that is thrown around so much you might feel it's lost a bit of its sparkle. But that's because you haven't met another one of our experts: our super-inspiring and super-gentle mental health nurse and mindfulness teacher, Lucy Livesey. Lucy knows all about the grief and heartache of baby loss and termination for medical reasons (TFMR) so we feel she's perfectly placed to offer this incredible mindfulness support – we could listen to her soothing voice all day. (S4, E5)

MINDFULNESS WITH LUCY LIVESEY

I have a background in psychiatric nursing, and I've been a nurse for nine years. I embarked on my mindfulness training when I lost my daughter, Ellie, at twenty-three weeks when I had a TFMR. I wanted to try something to help me with how I was feeling following her death, so I completed a four-year teacher training programme, which helped me create this free baby app called Ellie's Gift. Ellie's Gift is an app that encourages lots of techniques to promote comfort and relaxation and aims to reduce anxiety during the birth of a baby who has died.

Mindfulness saved me after Ellie died, so it was important to me to support parents who had to deliver babies who had also passed away. This would be Ellie's gift to the world.

A kind attitude: getting from A to B

The mindfulness I teach is about learning how to be with difficulty – so actively turning towards your suffering, but with a kind, non-judgemental attitude. When we grieve, it's very easy to try to push it away and box it up. But there is a very apt saying that goes: 'What we resist, persists.'

Let me give you an example: say someone is struggling with anxiety and they want to get from anxiety to a state of calm; if the letter A represents anxiety and B is calm, you have still got to be with A to get to B. That anxiety, if you resist it, only gets worse. And it's the same with grief.

The aim of mindfulness is to educate families to learn how to be with and around their experience of loss. Mindfulness helps us to stay in the present moment, which can be hard when we are grieving.

Trying not to think about the future is especially hard. We need to recognise when our minds run off into future years, e.g. how will we cope during the baby's anniversary or when our friends have babies? Living in the past is unhelpful too. When our minds jump back into the past it can be to a time when we regretted a decision that we made about our baby or wondered whether we looked after ourselves well enough during pregnancy. But these past and future thoughts are not real.

The practice

Mindfulness is a practice – it's not just a case of 'OK, I'll do a bit of mindfulness and then that's all better.' Mindfulness helps us to hold both our suffering and joy in a big container – you can't have one without the other. For many people, when they are grieving, they want to shut down and they don't welcome in joy in any way, but mindfulness helps us be aware of everything – and the wonderful side effect is that it helps us to relax. But it does take time and patience – it's not a quick fix. In fact, we are not trying to 'fix' anything at all. We have to learn how to be with grief, but it's about lessening the suffering. The fact that we have lost a baby is heart-wrenching enough without adding on the extra guilty thoughts of 'I should have done this' or 'Why didn't I do that?'

Mindfulness helps us to recognise when all these thought patterns come up, so not only can we say: 'Here's that bloody thought again,' but we register that we don't have to jump into that thought; that we can stay here with our breath, and we can let that thought come in and then go out again. It's not about getting rid of thoughts, because they will come back, but it's learning what to do with a head full of thoughts – thoughts that don't give you a break. It's a great practice and something that has helped me deal with Ellie's death.

A kind attitude

Mindfulness helps us to cultivate a sense of kindness and self-compassion. That's so important in grief, because we need to take time to drop the judgement, drop the guilt and allow ourselves to grieve without all the other stuff. The substance of mindfulness is so rich, but I know a lot of people who don't give it space because it feels a bit 'woo-woo'. I have heard from people that they don't want to try mindfulness because they aren't 'that kind of person' or simply say 'it's not my thing'. But all we are doing is focusing on your breath for a few minutes. And the practice starts there. You don't have to sit cross-legged on the floor; you don't have to start making humming noises; you don't have to be of a certain type of religion – it works for everyone!

Starting slow

Mindfulness isn't aimed at people who aren't ready to receive it. Asking somebody who is in the throes of grief or trauma to close their eyes and be with their breath might be extremely distressing for them. Equally, asking someone to do a 30-minute meditation when they've just lost a baby is impossible. You can't ask that of someone in that situation.

Mindfulness isn't about emptying your mind of thoughts either. I work with a lot of people who say, 'I can't empty my mind, it's impossible!'

But believe me when I say, I am definitely not trying to empty your mind. If I emptied your mind, you'd be dead! This is about holding joy and grief in the same container with kindness and non-judgement.

It allows us to notice the moment: OK, what emotion is here and what is going to help me in this moment? And when you acknowledge that emotion, you know that certain things will help elevate it – it might help you to ring a friend or self-soothe with a relaxing bath or pamper. This awareness gives us control so that our minds don't jump around and go completely berserk, which means you can't think straight.

So it's not about stopping the thoughts – it's about noticing what thoughts are showing up, but it stops there. It's like creating space between you and the thought.

The thought train

I'm able to notice when I am having thoughts that are distressing – we call it getting carried along by the thought train. The thought train tends to lead us to a crappy destination of self-loathing, shame and guilt, but if I can just learn to watch that thought train go through the tunnel, away from me, I realise I don't have to jump on it. They are just thoughts, and thoughts are not always true, so that in itself is very freeing.

Repeat after me: I am not that thought. Yes, acknowledge the thought, but then it's gone. All it wants is to be seen and heard, so you can give it space to be there, and then let it go on its way.

The baggage carousel

Ever stepped off an aeroplane, made it down to baggage reclaim and watched as the same suitcases go round and round on the carousel? This is a bit like our minds. Sometimes the same thoughts just keep going round and round in our heads. Some disappear and won't come back – someone has taken that suitcase off the conveyor belt – but some bags just keep doing the rounds. And as an observer, you can keep watching those thoughts. It's OK. You don't need to try to leap onto the belt and throw the suitcases off or try to stop the conveyor; you just need to see the bags and know that you are OK. It's about having authority over your pain, rather than letting your pain dominate you.

Three-minute breathing space practice

Because mindfulness is a practice, it's a good idea to start with something small like this – the three-minute breathing space. This is a short meditation that helps us to experience the present moment and reconnect with ourselves. This is helpful when we experience

---

negative thought patterns following baby loss, which only add to our suffering. It's a simple technique that is done in the following way:

1. **Attend to what is:** The first step invites you to attend broadly to your experience – note it, but without the need to change what is being observed.

2. **Focus on the breath:** The second step narrows the field of attention to a single, pointed focus on the breath in the body.

3. **Attend to the body:** The third step widens your attention again to include the body as a whole and any sensations that are present.

BEING GRATEFUL: WHAT DOES THAT REALLY MEAN?

Gratitude doesn't mean waking up and feeling full of thanks every day. It can be sparked by something as small as the sun shining through the clouds in the morning or the smell of clean sheets when you go to bed at night. See? It's not ground-breaking stuff. But you do have to work at it, and if you do, you'll have a source of gratitude each day. We find saying it out loud helps. Sending voice notes to each other is also one of our favourite ways of recognising, recording and sharing our gratitude.

When it comes to reconnecting with ourselves mentally, our lovely friend Charla Grant, founder of The Grateful Hearts Club, a place dedicated to understanding and celebrating the importance of gratitude (S2, E19), is the queen. Not only is she a baby loss warrior herself, she has helped others overcome some pretty heavy moments in their lives by reframing their thoughts, starting with the little things. It's unreal how inspiring she is and how strong her approach to gratitude is within the baby loss community, where it can, understandably, be so lost. We'll let her take the reins from here.

GRATITUDE WITH CHARLA GRANT

I'm naturally a positive person who can always see the goodness in things, so I went into each of my pregnancies always believing that everything would be OK, we would get there and we would get our happy ending. I clung onto that for a very long time – I had such belief! But, after experiencing our first miscarriage, I prepared myself for the worst and from that point I was always at war with myself about being both optimistic but realistic.

I have a unicornuate uterus (see page 273), so my uterus isn't the same shape as everyone else's. It's taken me a long time to say it with pride, because it's part of me and I no longer feel shame about the parts of me that are different. Besides, it has the word 'unicorn' in it, which makes me feel like it's the most special type of uterus. When you have a unicornuate uterus you only have half. You only have one fallopian tube instead of two and the last pregnancy I had was ectopic, so they had to take the only tube I had, and that meant that the chances of having a family naturally were taken with it.

Before our quest for a family finally ended with that ectopic pregnancy, I had also had an MMC and another ectopic pregnancy. Our daughter, Olive, was a successful pregnancy but she died in childbirth. Because my uterus was a lot smaller, she didn't have as much space to grow and, when she came at twenty-nine weeks, she wasn't strong enough to survive.

After my series of unsuccessful pregnancies and Olive's death, I lost the positive person I once was. On the outside I was very good at wearing a mask, smiling and nodding in all the right places and looking like I had it all together. But on the inside, I very much started to lose both hope and myself. I just existed. And when you have no hope, what is there? I was so focused on everything I didn't have, thinking things like: 'Having a baby is so easy for everyone else,' that I was lost in comparison for a long time.

I survived this dark time by putting one foot in front of the other, and I noticed that it really helped me if I could focus on just one small positive each day. When you are really lost in grief, these things can literally be tiny, but it was a way for my brain to help me make sense of living rather than just existing. I didn't read a book on it and think to myself, 'Oh, OK... I'm going to be grateful today.' On reflection, I realised that what I was thinking and doing was essentially gratitude, I just didn't have a label for it then. It was a tool I developed to help me through each day.

I call these little things CRUMBS OF JOY. When you are grieving, these small crumbs can give you that little bit of hope. Whether it's feeling the sun on your face, washing your hair, a smile from a stranger or hearing birds outside your window, noticing these things and acknowledging them a little bit in that moment helps you, in time, realise that there is still goodness in life. Joy feels too joyful when you are in the real depths of grief, but gratitude gives you a little moment to reflect on those small things. And when you start to notice the small things, the small things then add up and a really dark day can seem a bit lighter.

Habits form in lovely ways and, in time, rather than looking left or right in comparison, you notice the good stuff in your own life. If you can focus on what you have right there in front of you, it starts to feel bigger.

'Gratitude is a funny word, isn't it? It sounds really joyful, like I was skipping around, shouting out, "Everything's OK and all is happy!"'

When I was living through that dark time, for me to get through life I had to go right back to basics and think, 'OK, I have a husband, I am not alone, I have someone.' When you can feel like what you have in your life is 'enough', that is gratitude. It has taken me a long time and I have done a lot of work to understand myself and my grief. Gratitude for me has taken time and practice, but I think that's where the hope comes in. Understanding that your life is going to be different, you would always wish it another way, but that you can't change it. You have to learn to accept that and think that if there are any tiny crumbs which come out of what you've been through, then focusing on them is all you have.

When you have been through this kind of trauma – when you have all the love but no babies to love – it's hard to find a way of channelling that love somewhere else. My work with The Grateful Hearts Club gives me the opportunity to do that and to use that love for good, because it is endless. If you can find a way to do that – to turn your pain into love – then that can be really healing and can be a big part of your journey.

The gratitude exercise: crumbs of joy

What do your crumbs of joy look like? The biggest gift you can give yourself is to understand what can help a dark day seem a little brighter. Take some time to think about three small things that make you smile. Could you add them into your day? When they happen, take the time to notice them and mindfully engage with them. Being grateful in your joyful moments is a great way to add a little more gratitude. Remember, small joys really do add up.

RECONNECTING WITH YOURSELF PHYSICALLY

Louisa MacInnes, our certified sex and relationship Coach, is the fountain of all sexy time knowledge and is incredibly passionate about helping women reconnect with their bodies and reignite the flames of their inner sensual selves. It was love at first zoom for me (Bex) and we're really excited not only to feature her here, but also to have her as an expert in our courses. Strap in and read on, Louisa's bringing sexy back…

CONNECTING TO OUR BODY WITH LOUISA MACINNES

Connecting to our bodies might sound like a strange or negative thing to say, but let's get one thing straight: the relationship we have with ourselves is the most important one we can cultivate. No matter how much we might ask our partner or our best friend or our parents or our children to look after us and support us or meet our needs, there will always be a limit to what they can do. So we need to learn to look after ourselves. It's so powerful and it's such a grounding thing to step into.

It involves examining the relationship you have with your body both pre-loss and post-loss, and developing a feeling of love and acceptance towards it. I would describe it as like talking to your inner child and telling them, 'I've got you.' So what can you do to rebuild that sense of acceptance and love for yourself and your body?

Exercise: reconnecting (honestly) with your body

This exercise is about reconnecting with your body and understanding your relationship to it. The focus is on an honest acknowledgment of how you feel – good and bad – rather than trying to band-aid any difficult feelings with inauthentic 'positivity'. Awareness and acceptance of what is true for you means that any subsequent 'action' can be from a place of considered response rather than reaction.

Take off your clothes and stand naked in front of a full-length mirror.

- Starting with the top of your head, then going down your whole body, look in the mirror and tell yourself what you see and how it makes you feel.
- Express your vulnerabilities as well as an appreciation of the parts of your body you are most proud of.
- This may not be as easy as it seems. Allow yourself to feel any emotions you have and allow those emotions to be there.
- Close the exercise by giving yourself a hug.

Finding pleasure in your body

The most important thing to remember here is that finding pleasure in your body isn't – I repeat, *isn't* – rocket science. And it's not scary either. It can be as simple as giving yourself a massage. Get out your favourite body lotion. The one you are saving for some reason, but you can't quite remember why. Now, slowly and mindfully, put some lotion on your hands and give yourself a massage. Close your eyes and feel. If you want to help your libido, focus on your breasts to start with, helping you connect with a feeling of self-pleasure and self-love for your body. If you are ready to connect again with your genitals and your pleasure in a way that feels totally on your terms, you'll begin to realise that there is no pressure. There is no expectation on you at this moment – this isn't about making a baby or making your partner feel good about what he or she is doing; this is just about you.

Slow down. Really take time to turn yourself on. Notice what feels good. Take time to explore different types of touch on different parts of your body and genitals. Breathe! Move your body. You've got this.

The more you do this, the more you will be able to access where your pleasure is and identify what emotions may or may not be coming through. And when you start feeling ready to have sex with your partner again, having first prioritised your own self-pleasure will be invaluable.

Imagine this scenario: if you are having sex and for one reason or another your libido goes out the window or you go really dry or a thought has popped into your head and you want to feel turned on again, then if you know your body and you know what your body likes and dislikes, you have an incredible power. You don't have to expect your partner to be able to bring you back into that state of arousal; you can do it yourself. It's about knowing what your body needs in order to feel relaxed and more available for pleasure again.

Body love affirmations

Here at *TWGGE* we are all for short, sharp, simple reminders of how bloody marvellous our bodies really are, especially the battered and bruised ones that undergo pain, loss and confusion. Whether this is your bag or not, we're just going to leave some body-positivity affirmations right here for you to have a gander at. As always, sending love to you all…

- My body deserves love and respect.
- I am at home in my body.
- I choose to be kind to my body.
- I am grateful for what my body is capable of doing.
- I understand what my body might not be capable of doing.
- I trust and listen to my body.

'Affirmations motivate, inspire and encourage us to take action and realise our goals.'

THE GRATEFUL HEARTS CLUB

'Just because she carries it well, doesn't mean it isn't heavy.'

A treat for you (yes, you!)

We know how hard it is to invest in ourselves, especially when we are dealing with grief. We know women who have received vouchers for a massage from friends after suffering baby loss and, after the initial 'why-the-actual-f**k-do-I-want-to-be-treating-myself-at-a-time-like-this?' wore off, they appreciated the gesture. When we are feeling disconnected physically or emotionally, it's so easy for us to feel that we shouldn't be investing in ourselves, we shouldn't be loved, we shouldn't do anything that is kind to ourselves. But the reality is, you bloody well should. If you already have children when you suffer a loss, you have the added mother's guilt to go like a cherry on top of that self-indulgent feeling. But we can't continue to pour from an empty cup, even if the idea of taking time out or spending money on yourself seems like the most unnatural and inappropriate thing in the world. We're here to tell you, it's not. Bring out that massage voucher that was shoved in the back of the drawer. Send out a treatment credit to a friend in the baby-loss community and remind them that it's OK to show themselves some kindness when the time is right for them. They deserve it. You deserve it.

REASSESSING THE BLAME: TERMINATION FOR MEDICAL REASONS (TFMR)

We wanted to include a dedicated section within this chapter to TFMR, as it's a complete mind-f**k and can make it particularly difficult for sufferers to reconnect with themselves both mentally and physically. If you have made that heart-breaking decision not to carry on with your pregnancy due to serious health complications (and potentially a life risk for you or your baby)… where does that leave you? What boat do you sit in now? Miscarriage seems like the wrong vessel, yet you aren't pregnant either, and surely your vessel should be a rickety old beaten-up dinghy that has a neon sign above it so everyone knows to avoid it because, after all, you made that choice. Let us tell you something right now, once and for all: a TFMR is exactly that – a termination for a *medical reason*. We know from experience that it's especially hard to reconnect with ourselves physically when we initially feel so vividly let down by our bodies.

This four-letter acronym can't begin to explain the complications of such a baby loss. The feelings you have if you are told you need to end your pregnancy are just as valid, as strong and as painful as those in any other type of baby loss.

Take the time you need, get the support you need, and remember, you have an inner strength and resolve that you won't think is possible.

There is no judgement; there is no banishment; there is nothing but love and compassion for anyone going through this, because it can make you feel more alone and more abandoned than ever. Your body hasn't failed your baby and you haven't failed your baby. You are one of the strongest warriors in this outfit, because you have had to stand up and say, 'I am making the best decision I can with the information I have. I understand that this isn't going to work. I understand that my body hasn't done anything wrong. I need love and understanding, but this must come from within me first. I am a brave, beautiful soul and I am ready.'

We are here for you.

*

Claire Hall was a few years below me (Laura) at school. We kept in touch and I remember knowing that she was pregnant and then finding out that she lost her baby. I never knew the circumstances until I was more open about my own experiences and she got in touch. Despite the guilt she felt, she wanted to share her story of TFMR, knowing the positive impact it would have for those going through the same situation.

CLAIRE'S STORY

'The weight of the decision and the guilt of terminating my baby kept me silent and full of shame.'

I had a termination for medical reasons in my third trimester of pregnancy. After measuring a bit big during a routine midwife appointment, I was sent for an ultrasound and abnormalities were detected in my baby. Her skull had prematurely fused due to a genetic condition called Apert syndrome. As a result, her brain hadn't developed properly and, as another part of the condition, her fingers and toes were fused together like mittens.

Although people live with Apert syndrome, our baby's condition appeared severe. The doctors couldn't tell us with certainty how compromised her life would be, and while part of me wanted to be hopeful that our baby wouldn't be too badly affected, we had to accept that she would certainly require multiple and ongoing surgeries – a life we did not want for our child.

We decided to terminate our pregnancy and end our baby's life before it had begun. The process of having a termination and, days later, giving birth to our baby was filled with terror. The termination involved passing a long needle through my tummy into my baby's heart to stop it. I'd been told that if this didn't work, they'd have to try 'less humane' alternatives. I lay there praying for it to work and for my baby to die, as I was terrified of the alternative.

Giving birth to her took days, as my body fought to keep the baby it wasn't ready to deliver yet. She arrived silently and although I'm grateful to have photos of us together, only I know how much of a fraud I felt looking lovingly at a baby I was scared of, with her poorly misshapen head and fused fingers and toes. I wish I could put my arms around that woman and tell her she doesn't have to be so brave. That she doesn't deserve this.

The weight of the decision and the guilt of terminating my baby kept me silent and full of shame. I was desperate to sweep it under the carpet and distance myself from the pain and sadness. Even within the baby-loss community, I felt totally disconnected and unable to relate to anyone because our choice made me feel dirty and bad. I didn't fit into any category of baby loss, as (due to how far along in pregnancy I was) our daughter is legally recorded as stillborn, even though we'd opted for a TFMR. I felt like a cheat using the word 'stillbirth'.

Returning to work, I felt unable to meet people's eye as they asked how my baby was doing, fearful of their judgement that I'd chosen to terminate because our baby wasn't perfect. I later realised that those voices of judgement I feared so much were my own – the ones that bring on the shame and guilt, and tell us we don't deserve to honour our baby because we ultimately ended her life.

I found freedom in speaking my truth and honouring my daughter Evelyn in small, everyday ways. Advice from a dear friend that I still use to this day is 'to use the language that brings most meaning to your baby'. I have had two precious daughters since Evelyn, but increasingly I want to include her when talking about my children. Evelyn, my first born, is part of me, forever.

Claire Hall (S1, E10)

*

Having a TFMR is something we discuss a lot in our podcasts, but one piece of advice that has stuck with us is from Lucy Livesey and involves writing a letter to your future self. This letter should explain how you came to your decision and reinforces that you made the best decision you could with the information you had at the time. This may help you reaccept that decision in the years to come.

Chapter 8

Trying Again and Pregnancy After Loss

*'The unbelievable strength of a mother's love can be seen
in a woman trying to conceive after loss.'*

Following the loss of a baby, there is no right or wrong time to start trying again. Some couples want to start the process straight away; others need time off, time to heal as a pair. Sometimes one half of a couple wants to hold off, while the other wants to try again immediately. This can cause pain and discord – visit Chapter 5 on Family Relationships for some tips on how to keep communication going.

For so many of us, the fear of the positive pregnancy test is huge. In fact, the fear and apprehension surrounding 'trying again' after loss is huge. Who knew that trying for a baby in the future might potentially involve trauma and anxiety rather than desire and passion? Who knew that periods would be triggering; that sex would be pressured; that our behaviour would become obsessive, erratic, emotional? This crock of shit is what TTC (trying to conceive) after loss looks like for so many of us. A frightening void of uncertainty.

When our babies die, we lose so much more than a child. We lose more, even, than our hopes and dreams of a life with that child. We lose the excitement and joy that surrounded TTC and pregnancy before we knew what could happen – what *did* happen.

Sex can become emotional for the wrong reasons; it can feel cloaked in sadness, or it can feel desperate and functional. Every month can become an emotional roller coaster – even more so than in the TTC journey before loss – an internal battle of hope and fear.

We know that we desperately desire to be pregnant, but we also know the unbearable pain and heartbreak that we went through on the journey to have a baby last time.

So, what do we do? How do we get around or over this? Unfortunately, not only is the answer personal, differing from woman to woman, couple to couple, but there's no concrete solution.

When you're TTC, your life goes on hold. You *always* know where you are in your cycle. Whether it's pre-ovulation, the magic five-day fertile window, the mind-f**k that is the TWW (two-week wait) or the disappointment when Aunt Flo and cycle-day one roll round again.

IT. IS. EXHAUSTING.

It also turns you into someone/something you don't recognise. Maybe you're taking three ovulation tests a day because you're paranoid you'll miss the window. Perhaps you're checking your cervical mucus in public.[2]

You find yourself avoiding anything that might possibly cause conflict during your fertile window, because an argument might mean sex is off the table (figuratively speaking...).

You make certain to hop on the good foot and do the bad thing

---

2   Listen to S1, E12 of the podcast to hear about the time Bex checked her CM on a camping trip. It's a great story.

every single day during that window – until sex is the least sexy thing you can think of.

And then you wait... you google every ache, twinge, emotion and response you have in the following two weeks. Forgot to lock the front door? You're googling 'forgetfulness as an early sign of pregnancy'.

And then you start testing. You test at eight days past ovulation, even though you know that it will be negative whether conception has occurred or not. You test again and again until you've spent over £50 on preggo tests. You get angry and throw them away – only to return and peel off the banana skin ten minutes later to check in a different light...

You have to hide them all from your other half because you know he'd think you're batshit crazy. You google 'batshit crazy behaviour... sign of pregnancy?'

To all of you on your TTC-after-loss journey – we see you.

'Every month I'm terrified of seeing a negative pregnancy test, but I'm terrified of seeing a positive too...'

The fact of the matter is, when we have passed the stage of 'ooh, we'll just let it happen', the pressure during the fertile window is huge. Night after night of shagging (at least five in a row) becomes about as sexy as the thought of BoJo in Speedos. Nope, it just ain't happening.

The truth is, TTC sex sometimes isn't sexy. You get to the point where you and your partner are on a countdown to the end of the fertility window just so you can have a breather. And sometimes rumpy pumpy is off the cards for the rest of the month because, let's face it, a) you're not a machine and b) it could be viewed as 'pointless' or a 'waste'.

All this crap is not good for you or your partner and will most probably get you down and start causing resentments. But, once again, this is absolutely standard. It's totally ordinary to feel this way.

So, if you find yourself needing a little reassurance in this area, look no further than our Sex and Relationship Coach, Louisa MacInnes. It's not just about sex when it comes to TTC; it's all about laying bare (sorry, we couldn't help it) and stripping back (we are so the giggly idiots at the back of biology class) your relationship with your partner before a knicker has even been flung. What we love about Louisa's approach is that this has to work for *you* – not your friends, not anyone else, just you. We'll let her explain.

LOUISA MACINNES' ADVICE FOR REBUILDING SEXUAL INTIMACY

My suggested approach is split into four parts. The first is all about coming back to our own bodies – reconnecting with them and rediscovering our relationship with our erotic self. The second step is about communication with your partner – the language you use and how you listen. The third step is about rediscovering what it is that connects you and your partner – the shared values and the differences that can be celebrated. The fourth step is then bringing all of that to the bedroom, feeling safe and in control.

Let's go through it step by step:

1. Pleasure in our bodies
It's worth repeating here that everyone's experience of baby loss and miscarriage is different, so there is a huge landscape of emotion involved. Some of you might feel disappointment in your bodies, or detachment, numbness, a lack of confidence, a lack of desire… these are all normal emotions. This first step is about coming back to understanding and trusting our relationship with our bodies again. Reframing and rebuilding a relationship with our physical self and allowing ourselves to access pleasure is discussed more in Chapter 7.

2.   Communicate

When a couple has experienced baby loss or miscarriage, even though they have had a shared experience, they won't necessarily have the same perspective or response to it. It's important for couples to understand that however long they have been together, they might not necessarily feel the same way about something – and that's OK. Sometimes there is a huge amount of frustration around that. It can feel lonely and alienating when the one person we expect to feel the same as us seems to be having a different experience.

However, if we can learn to honour those differences, get curious about them and be willing to communicate in a way that welcomes all perspectives, then we can create a foundation for greater connection, love and empathy. Here are a few points to bear in mind:

Respect: A lot of relationship challenges are based on frustration, when our partner doesn't seem to be hearing or understanding our perspective. You're having a difficult conversation or argument and all you are thinking about is what you are going to say in your defence. Sound familiar? But this can quickly become a battle of wills, a game of attack and defend, wherein there can really be 'no winner' and the core need – simply wanting to be heard or understood – can rarely be met. But communication is about learning how to really listen and allow each other that space.

The wall of shit: I like to use this as a way of explaining how resentments can build up between a couple. Visualise a clean pane of glass standing between two people. What can often happen is that little petty resentments, such as who takes out the bins or who does the housework, can get built up over time. Now imagine these petty resentments are like bits of dirt or shit getting thrown at this pane of glass. And then, after a while, it's not clear or see-through anymore. It becomes thick with dirt and mud to the point where you can't really see or hear each other anymore – there's just this massive wall of accumulated resentment that becomes really hard to break through. Try the exercise 'Actively talking and actively listening' on page 201 to develop a communication structure that can really help both to wipe down that pane of glass and to get into a pattern of communication where each party feels safe enough to know their feelings will be understood, if not always shared.

<u>Love languages:</u> There is an interesting concept around love languages and how people speak to each other. One partner might really feel loved when their partner gives words of affirmation; for example, 'I really believe in you,' or 'You were amazing when you were doing that the other day,' or 'I am really proud of you.' This is what some people need to hear to feel the love from their partner. Whereas for other people, those words would have less impact than if their partner performed an act of service, such as cooking dinner or sorting out house admin without being asked. From this perspective, making your partner feel loved is about understanding each other's love language and learning it, especially if it's not the same as yours. Communication is about being seen and being heard.

3.   Prioritising time spent together

It's important to come back to the values and commonalities that brought you and your partner together in the first place. What attracted you to each other? How did you spend your time? What made you want to have a baby? It's important to prioritise time and fun and pleasure and connection and intimacy outside of the bedroom, if that is what we're hoping for inside the bedroom, otherwise it's going to be hard to suddenly turn it on when it comes to having sex – either for fun or for making babies.

4. Intimacy

When it comes to sex, the first thing to consider is: how do we deal with the fact that there will be a massive elephant in the room? Sex when you are trying to conceive – even if you haven't experienced baby loss – can feel unsexy, robotic, formulaic and more about getting the job done than experiencing pleasure. When you then add in baby loss, it's additionally fraught and emotional.

EXERCISES TO TRY

When it comes to sex after loss and trying to conceive again, there is no magic solution. There is no quick fix. The exercises Louisa has outlined here offer little steps that mark a commitment to yourself and your partner, with the biggest challenge being to remember to do them. There is sometimes a sense that we live in a quick-fix society – we order something and it comes the next day, or we have a problem and think, 'Quick, I need to solve it!' But actually, this stuff takes time. And don't think that because you might have done an eye-gazing exercise you will suddenly be super-connected to your partner and everything will be brilliant. All these exercises might help, but they won't eradicate the anxiety or the fear or the sadness.

ACTIVELY TALKING AND ACTIVELY LISTENING

Take it in turns to speak for three to five minutes about something that is niggling you. How familiar does this sound? 'You never take the bins out. You are so selfish. You don't think about…' They are all default ways of falling into an argument. Using the accusatory 'you' and big words like 'always and never' makes it easy for your partner to reply with, 'Well, actually, I took the bins out last week,' and therefore the whole argument becomes a very futile way of getting a point across.

Try using 'I' statements instead. So, for example, 'When you don't take the bins out, I feel like the majority of the housework is left to me and that makes me feel frustrated and undervalued.' You are then, as the person using 'I' statements, owning the experience.

The person who is listening plays a vital part in this process. It's not about defending or excusing or even responding to what the person is saying in a solution-orientated way. It's more about acknowledgment, so: 'OK, I hear what you're saying – that when I don't take the bins out, it makes you feel like I don't care about you or I take you for granted.' The only way the person who is listening should respond is to clarify their understanding of what is being shared/expressed – to show they have understood what has been said, even if they don't agree with it.

And then you swap over, so the person who is listening has a chance to talk, and the talker has a chance to actively listen. The idea is not to talk about the same thing, so the person now talking focuses on something other than the bins. And again, it's not about whether what each person is saying is true or not to the listener; it's about talking so you are heard and keeping quiet so you can listen.

This is a really useful tool to practise and get comfortable with when addressing the small, petty, 'annoying-but-no-real-biggie' stuff between you. Then, with practice, it is something you can draw on when having deeper, more difficult conversations as well – about grief or challenges with sex after baby loss. You will have cultivated the ability to really listen and be curious about each other's experience, and you will have built a foundational understanding that what is true for us may not be true for another and that's OK. You will be holding space for your own experience as well as your partner's, and in doing so you will be creating the basis for greater connection.

BOSSY MASSAGE

This exercise is good for working on intimacy and communication. You take it in turns to give each other a massage. The person who is receiving the massage must direct the touch of the person doing the massage, saying things in a very direct manner, such as, 'Can you massage my right thigh?' Or, 'Can you do that a bit harder on my shoulder?' Or, 'Stroke my foot.' This can feel like a bit of a clunky and strange exercise when you first start doing it, but it can have lots of benefits – it encourages the person who is receiving the massage to drop out of the thinking mind and into the feeling body, to identify what feels good and, crucially, to ask for it.

This exercise is really valuable for the person giving the massage too. Sometimes with sex, we think we should automatically know what we are doing, that our partners are mind readers and that what worked last time will work again today. We also often forget to actually talk during sex!

But how does it feel to receive feedback and instructions? As much as we have been conditioned to think otherwise, sex is not a performance. I repeat, sex is *not* a performance. This is a collaborative exercise, because sex is a collaborative experience. Swap roles and try being the one offering the massage and being directed so you get to learn the tools for each role.

This exercise gives you both a connection to what feels good and helps you ask for what feels good, give your partner what they want and respond to what your partner needs. This is important when it comes to sex after loss because you might feel scared, or you might feel extra emotional, but the more you feel that you are in control of your body, that your needs are important and that you're safe to express them, the more likely you are to be able to let go, experience pleasure, enjoy sex and want more of it in the future.

EYE GAZING

This exercise is pretty much what it says on the tin – you are essentially looking into each other's eyes in silence.

Facing each other, consciously slow down your breathing and try to synchronise it with your partner's – so you are breathing in together and breathing out together. Try to maintain eye contact throughout, and allow any emotions that may surface to be there. It can be useful to set a timer for this so you can drop the exercise without wondering when it will end! Even three minutes would be enough. Just do what feels achievable.

Breathing and being together can be really connecting, as well as emotional, because you are really looking at each other and you are not being distracted. Of course, in the beginning it can make you feel really awkward and uncomfortable, but once you get through it, there is a sense of literally being 'seen', which is really, really powerful.

HITTING THE RESET BUTTON

It's very easy to go on autopilot when you have been with the same partner for a while, by which we mean that sex can be a bit like sex by numbers. Predictable. Samey. A little dull. But one very quick and very easy way to reset this is to focus on your physical sensations – the touch of your hand on their body. The texture of their skin. The areas of their body that feel smooth or rough, cool or warm, firm or soft. Slow down your touch and really notice these sensations. And vice versa, notice how it feels to be touched all over your body. Not only will it increase your receptivity to pleasure, but the more you know what you like, the more you will know what to ask for in the future. It's a win-win. So go forth and feel.

SEX ALL MONTH ROUND

This isn't an exercise as such (well, technically it is exercise, of course) but a reminder that there was probably a time in your relationship when sex wasn't about setting the scene, or the context, or feeling relaxed; it was just about having 'a quickie'. And that's OK! Don't deny the fact that sex doesn't always need to be immensely pleasurable, really amazing and intricately thought-out.

Having sex outside of your ovulatory window is important because then sex becomes more about sex again and not just about trying to conceive and the pressure that brings. If you can keep sex going throughout the month, it's going to support you when you need to have sex when you are ovulating. For both of you, keeping the fire gently burning rather than trying to turn it on and off again will make a big difference.

TRYING AGAIN

We love Louisa. We call her our sexpert or sexologist basically because we love those names. We hope her advice in this chapter might help you bring back some fun to what can be a very challenging and anxious experience. We know what it's like. And so does Jane Moscardini, who we first met following her experience of a TFMR. She was in the midst of TTC, and not only is she a beautiful person who was very open and vulnerable during the podcast recording (we all cried numerous times, even Laura with her stone-cold heart), but just try saying her surname with an exaggerated Italian accent and tell us you don't love her even more!

JANE'S STORY

'The more I say, "Actually, it's my second pregnancy — we lost our first child but we're OK and we're hopeful," the easier it is. But it takes lots of practice, so be patient with yourself.'

My first pregnancy started to go wrong at my nineteen-week cervix check when the sonographer noticed something wasn't right with my baby's brain. Then, after weeks of scans, blood tests, an MRI and an amniocentesis, we were told that the most likely prognosis was that our baby boy, Archie, had an extremely rare genetic condition that had caused his brain to fill with fluid and thus prevented any further growth or development. The doctors didn't think Archie would survive the pregnancy, and if he did, he would have to be born early because his head was large and would continue to swell due to the fluid on his brain. Our consultant was unsure of how much pain he would be in once he was born and also how long he would be able to survive outside of my womb. The team discussed all of the options we had and in the end, after lots of tears, we felt a TFMR would cause Archie the least amount of suffering. I gave birth to my first-born child and we got to meet him and hold him before saying our official goodbyes at his funeral a month later.

Fifteen months after Archie's death, myself and my partner felt as though we were strong enough to consider trying again. We both still longed to raise a child, and at thirty-seven years old I felt that waiting any longer would just put even more stress and pressure on me. After feeling ill one Tuesday afternoon and three pregnancy tests later, it finally sank in that I was pregnant. This is the point when friends and family think everything will be OK – you'll get your rainbow baby and everything will be wonderful – but, in reality, this is when the waiting game begins. It's hard to explain to people how you feel when you get pregnant after a loss. Of course, you feel grateful that you're even pregnant, but the trauma and fear are overwhelming, and the terror of not bringing another child home is often too much to bear.

Here's how I have come to explain my fear of pregnancy: imagine you have never been on a boat and the first time you ever got on a boat, it sank and you thought you were going to drown. And then the person you were with on that boat died, but you somehow managed to crawl to the shore and survive. Then a few months later someone says to you, 'I have a beautiful boat, do you want to come on an incredible trip with me?' And, of course, you don't want to because the only memory you have of being on a boat is horrifically traumatic.

Being pregnant again has allowed me to deal with the trauma I hadn't dealt with, along with bringing up a whole host of new situations that I've learnt to navigate. No one you know may understand what it's like to carry a child and not know if it will end with you arranging their funeral rather than organising a welcome-home party, and that is incredibly tough. Until I knew that my second baby wouldn't have the genetic condition my first had, I couldn't really invest in the pregnancy. I didn't want to fully open myself up to it.

People will also ask you if you have children or if this is your first pregnancy, and this can be very difficult because the answer is complicated and not easy to explain in a yes-or-no format. As a parent, I feel guilty if I don't mention the baby I lost because it feels as though I am denying their existence. For me, the more I say, 'Actually, it's my second pregnancy – we lost our first child but we're OK and we're hopeful,' the easier it is. But it takes lots of practice, so be patient with yourself.

Jane Moscardini (S3, E10 and 11)

THE DECISION TO STOP TRYING FOR A BABY DOESN'T MEAN THE BABY WASN'T WANTED

We have spoken to lots of folk in our *TWGGE* community about trying to conceive again after loss, as this is a subject that comes up a lot. There are some weird and wacky myths out there that if you want a baby badly enough, you will have one. If you follow the advice from Great-aunt Margaret about drinking unicorn piss on the third day of every month while sitting under an oak tree, you will have a baby in your arms in no time. However well meaning the advice from GA Maggie, it is often the fear of not knowing *if* and *when* it will ever happen that leaves us in a state of anxiety about our path to parenthood. GA Maggie can't predict the future – no one can!

Just as we believe it takes a huge amount of courage to keep trying for a baby, we also believe it takes a huge amount of courage to make the decision not to.

The pain of not knowing

I always said that, had I known that it would take seven years to start our family, then I could have enjoyed my time waiting. For me, it was the not knowing if we'd ever make it to parenthood that took its toll on me and us as a couple. With each year that went by, and each loss that we experienced, our desperation got more intense and life became sadder. To keep going through all of this, to keep trying, was the toughest thing I've ever had to do. I felt like giving up many times. I wish I'd known the end of the story, as it would have made living through the horror so much easier. If only we'd had a crystal ball, eh?

Laura

There are so many factors in the decision to stop trying for a baby: relationship pressures, finances, mental health, age, career… the list is endless and exhausting to consider. We hear about fertility treatments and donor eggs and surrogacy and adoption, but these aren't necessarily for everyone. Each course of action comes with its own unique set of circumstances and issues. Everyone's situation is different, and you cannot judge or be judged. As we've said before, judgement has no place here.

Choosing to stop doesn't mean failure. This will be the hardest decision you ever have to make, and it comes with its own immense grief that might take a lifetime to overcome. We are sending so much love to all of you who are contemplating this decision every day.

PREGNANCY AFTER LOSS

There is a common misconception that when we become pregnant after losing a baby, we breathe a huge sigh of relief. 'Phew,' we think. 'We can put that whole baby-loss business behind us now.' This is absolutely not the case, for many, many reasons.

Firstly, while we know that a new pregnancy may result in us taking home a longed-for baby, we also know that it might… not. We are all too familiar with what can and does go wrong during pregnancy, because we've been there. We've lived it. And this knowledge makes a pregnancy very difficult to enjoy or even accept. A very common coping mechanism is to deny the existence of the baby until he or she arrives safely. This means we don't do any of the exciting/

energising stuff that is so much part of pregnancy. We don't download the apps and work out due dates; we don't buy all the bumf; we don't spend hours planning names, looking up star signs or asking our friends to predict weights and dates.

Sam Woolford's story perfectly demonstrates that quagmire of emotions of pregnancy after loss. What can we say about Sam other than that when he shaved his head he looked like a big toe? Sam, aka Big Toe, was introduced to us by his lovely wife Emily, and he made us laugh and cry. He earnt the name Big Dog Ledge because his work with Sands United FC – a charity group of football teams for bereaved dads – is so inspirational. He has helped build a platform for men to share their experiences and he has done so in such a welcoming and down-to-earth way. He is an honorary member of *TWGGE* and has done everything we want to do – but for men.

SAM'S STORY

'Pregnancy after loss was way harder than we thought it would be. I think we really thought it would be a case of us finally healing, and it's definitely not. I don't feel any less sad about losing my daughter because I have had another son. That's just nonsense.'

When our first son, Ezra, was one and a half years old, we found out we were pregnant with our second child. At the twenty-week scan, we discovered we were having a little girl and that she had a congenital heart defect.

To start with, the diagnosis was very bad and it was unlikely she would make it into her teens – and she would have to have multiple surgeries to get to that point. But as the pregnancy progressed, her prognosis got better and, although she would still need to have some major surgeries, they would be straight-forward (in the context that open-heart surgery on an infant is). She was a very healthy weight when she was born, and they said we could go home for a few months to allow her to get bigger and better for surgery.

Unfortunately, on day five, our daughter started developing breathing problems and they had to bring forward the surgery. When she was ten days old, she had open-heart surgery, a triple bypass, and was in theatre for thirteen hours. The surgery went well and the prognosis was still good, even though she was on a ventilator until day sixteen. But the next day she had a cardiac arrest and was placed on a life-support machine, and she never recovered. We took her off life support on 23 December.

It was a total cluster-f**k of emotions: shock, disbelief, pure guttural sadness, anger, confusion, fear. And we had to explain to our son, who by that point was nearly two, why his sister wasn't coming home again. We were trying to deal with our grief in those following weeks and not doing a great job at it. When my wife fell pregnant later – which wasn't planned – we were barely even coping and, in all honesty, we were 90 per cent terrified and 10 per cent happy. We cried a lot initially, as we didn't know how to feel, but slowly we started to get excited again. When we miscarried at eleven weeks, it just felt like the biggest kick in the teeth ever.

A while later, we decided we did want to have another child and making that decision was a big leap, to actively try again. When my wife found out she was pregnant but then miscarried the next day, I hit rock bottom. I went off the rails a bit: I withdrew from the family, I wasn't talking to anyone and I was getting physically ill. I stopped playing with my son and I got very angry at things he did that were very normal toddler behaviours. I wasn't a nice person to be around, and my wife, knowing that this wasn't me, said I needed to sort my issues out. She told me about Sands United FC, football teams around the UK that are made up of bereaved fathers. We had tried a few support groups, but they were very female-focused. At first, I used any excuse not to go – the main problem being that the nearest team were based a long distance from where we lived. But my wife said that wasn't good enough, so I contacted them and I have started a new team here in my area.

My wife fell pregnant again and we now have another little boy called Reuben, our rainbow baby. I would be lying if I told you I didn't find that pregnancy incredibly hard, as did my wife. Pregnancy after loss was way harder than we thought it would be. I think we really thought it would be a case of us finally healing, and it's definitely not. It's separated into two things: we are exclusively happy about Reuben – he is wonderful and we love him – but he brings up loads of other things to do with Etta, our daughter, and the loss, and those things are not mutually exclusive. He has no bearing on the sadness, but he brings up the memories.

When we had our pregnancy after loss, we had people say to us, 'Oh, you don't seem very happy!' And that made us feel bad or guilty about the fact that we were feeling not exclusively happy. And it happened all the way through the pregnancy, with comments like, 'Oh, you've got to the twelve-week scan – are you allowed to be happy yet?' And I'd be like, 'No! I am still terrified.' It will never stop. We know what suffering is out there and we are trying our hardest to fight our anxieties, but it will never go away.

Sam Woolford (S3, E7), Sands United FC: www.sands.org.uk

EARLY SCANS

Pregnancy loss can also trigger huge anxieties surrounding scans. Before loss we look forward to a scan, thinking of it simply as an opportunity to see our baby for the first time. The black-and-white grainy image of a miracle. But those of us who have experienced MMC (missed miscarriage) find ourselves hyperventilating or sobbing in waiting rooms. We know what a scan can show and, devastatingly, what it might not show. And this puts huge emotional pressure and strain on an event that should be a wonderful milestone in our pregnancy journey.

Scanxiety is real

During the pregnancy of my 'rainbow baby', I booked an early 'reassurance' scan. In the waiting room, I sobbed. As I lay down on the bed in the darkened room, I couldn't breathe for fear of what I might be told. My heart was in my ears and I felt physically sick. I explained to the sonographer what had happened during my last scan, and she was lovely; she gave me all the time I needed and she was able to confirm as quickly as possible that our baby had a heartbeat. It was a wonderful moment, of course, but the atmosphere of that room – the sounds, the sights – flooded me with memories of my beautiful baby whose heart had stopped beating.

Bex

Extra ultrasound scans won't guarantee anything or predict how your pregnancy will progress, but it may give you some peace of mind. If you do want an early scan, you can talk to your GP or Early Pregnancy Unit, although it isn't always possible to have one. If you've previously had an ectopic pregnancy (see page 259), you should be offered a scan at six to eight weeks to check that the baby is developing in the right place. If you have had a molar pregnancy (see page 264), inform your GP, as you should also be entitled to an early scan. You're unlikely to be offered a scan any earlier than six weeks into your pregnancy because before then the sonographer won't be able to see anything conclusive.

Chris Binnie's experience of trying again after baby loss illustrates perfectly what an intense rollercoaster of emotions it can be. For the first three parts of Chris's story, head back to Chapters 1 (page 39), 4 (page 120) and 5 (page 130).

CHRIS'S STORY, PART FOUR

'I never, ever contemplated that we would go home with our twin girls. We didn't have any prams; we didn't have any cots – we had nothing. I had taken a cot back and I never, ever wanted to do that again.'

Trying to get pregnant again is a whole different challenge because you must psych yourself up for it in a lot of ways. We tried to get IVF on the NHS but because we had conceived Henry naturally, even though it was a stillbirth, we had ruled ourselves out of IVF, which is a brutal reality. Also, my wife was outside of the age bracket, which was thirty-five years old – she was forty-six years old.

We were trying to get an exemption to go outside of the criteria and I was so angry as we sat down with the fertility consultant because I believed we should be allowed one cycle of IVF on the NHS – of course we should, our baby died! But then he said something that totally changed my perspective on it all, which was that, although our situation was entirely tragic, everybody who comes through his door is a special case. If they weren't, they wouldn't be there.

It changed my perspective on what the focus for fertility treatment was – it wasn't about whether you had a stillbirth, it was about whether or not you could get pregnant. We had been trying, but nothing had happened. Ten months after Henry was born, my wife was diagnosed with breast cancer. And it turns out you do get IVF on the NHS when you are diagnosed with breast cancer, because they need to get you through it before you start your treatment.

They needed to harvest the eggs in order to start chemo, so we did that, and in the end there were three viable embryos that they froze. But then they said, with the cancer she had, if it was going to come back it would come back in two years, so you are going to have to wait two years because the last thing you want is for you to get pregnant and your cancer to come back.

We waited two years. And my wife beat cancer – which was amazing, of course – and we defrosted the embryos, but they didn't work. And then you have to pick yourself up again.

I know statistically IVF isn't always the magic answer. You are rolling the dice with IVF – you know you are potentially destined for more disappointment – but we decided to have one last try. After a lot of research, we went out to Cyprus for that. With IVF, you can test whether you are pregnant after two weeks, so at two weeks we knew we were.

Anyone who has experienced pregnancy after loss might also have found this, but the only reference point I had then was that, at some point, this baby is going to die. As soon as I saw a positive pregnancy test, I thought, 'At some point this is going to go wrong. I don't know when, but there is no way we will get a happy ending,' because our only experience was that when we get pregnant, babies die.

The whole mindset of pregnancy after baby loss is completely different. Every day I was thinking, 'Can we just get through this day? Can this baby just be alive to the end of this day? And then the next day.'

When my wife was just under eight weeks – and two days before we were due to see the fertility team – she had a massive bleed. We went to the hospital and into the scan room and the sonographer said, 'Everything looks OK. There is the first one, there is the second one.' For me, that encapsulates pregnancy after loss because, in the space of three and a half seconds, we went from waiting to be told what we had already decided in our head – which was that our baby had died – to being told everything is fine and you are having twins.

My wife was admitted to hospital at twenty-eight weeks with pre-eclampsia, and they said they would try to get her up to thirty-two weeks (which was a less scary way of saying we will probably just try to get you through the next two days), but in the end they got her up to thirty-four weeks, which is incredible – especially for twins. The girls were born at thirty-four weeks, and I genuinely didn't believe we would bring them home until we walked into theatre when they were delivered. That was the first point when I thought, 'This is going to be OK,' and that is because of my experience in operating theatres, which told me that if anything went really badly wrong, we were now in the room where the team could do whatever they needed to do. Until that point, I never, ever contemplated that we would go home with our twin girls. We didn't have any prams; we didn't have any cots – we had nothing. We hadn't let ourselves buy any of it. I had taken a cot back and I never, ever wanted to do that again, so we just didn't buy them. I think that offers a bit of a window onto the psychological side of pregnancy after loss and shows the refusal to accept that things might be OK. All your naivety, all your innocence, has gone.

Chris Binnie (S2, E11 and 12)

CONTROL THE CONTROLLABLES

One of our favourite sayings is *'control the controllables'*. There is so much in our lives that we do not have any control over, and this can be overwhelming when it comes to pregnancy after loss. A good way to combat feelings of panic and being overwhelmed is to practise control where we can. For example, we can control what we eat, what time we go to bed and the amount of social media we look at. Focus on nourishing yourself emotionally and physically, rather than getting caught up in what cannot be changed.

A new pregnancy and baby will never, ever replace what we have lost. We don't just lose our baby when we experience baby loss. We lose a part of ourselves that will remain nestled with that baby, and nothing can, will or should replace that.

'Pregnancy after loss is not necessarily a relief.'

When you experience recurrent miscarriage, you can sometimes be told by doctors just to keep trying. This, as someone told us once, is like running into the trenches with your eyes closed. It's so unknown. When you begin your fertility journey and you have one miscarriage, you have no idea whether it was just 'one of those things' or whether you might be a 'recurrent miscarriage sufferer'. The pain of miscarriage and baby loss is so utterly horrendous, you will ask if you are really willing put yourself through it again.

And you have the added unknown of whether your partner is willing to do it again too. 'We can try again, can't we? We can try again. We must try again...' Then there's the guilty feeling that, if you try again too quickly or hastily, your baby will be looking down on you thinking, 'Oh, she didn't really want me then, she just wants a baby...'

So it's yet another situation where you feel all the feels – guilt, desperation, frustration. And then there is the lack of confidence. When we lose our babies, we lose our confidence by the absolute bucketload. Confidence in ourselves. Confidence in our reproductive organs and our abilities to function 'correctly' as women; confidence in the world; confidence in society around us; confidence in the medical profession. We sometimes lose confidence in our partners, our friends and family – the ones who have always managed to make things better before. And we lose confidence in the future and our plans for it – this wasn't meant to happen, so how can we be sure of anything ever again? This is not healthy. But we are here. We have got you.

Chapter 9

Educating
Others

'The more we can completely dismantle the idea of "normal"
when it comes to women's bodies, the better.'

The whole 'fertility' aspect of our bodies, our inner parts and workings, are such a mystery to us. First, when we are young, our period is nothing more than an unwelcome inconvenience, ruining nights out and holidays, not to mention decent knickers and PJs.

Then we reach a stage where a split condom or a missed pill has us running to the chemist for the morning-after pill, cheeks aglow. Or we weren't careful 'enough' one month, or there was so much wine and... was there protection?! The morning Aunt Flo shows up, we exhale huge sighs of relief. What a close call!

Oh, those days – those blissfully ignorant days – when our sexual worries consisted only of STIs and fanny farts!

Then we get there, we're ready. We abandon the birth control, buy books on what to eat, how much to exercise and when in your cycle to have sex if you want a girl.

And then... and then...

Looking back on the hopes and fears we had can make us feel so foolish. The care we took *not* to get pregnant; how we took our fertility for granted; how we naively thought it would be so easy. We can't change the past, we can't talk to our yesterself and calm them down; we can only live in the here and now, doing what is right, and safe, and good for us in the moment.

And of course, we can teach, we can educate and support, and we can provide resources for the next generation of women who face the pain of infertility and baby loss.

FIVE THINGS THEY DON'T TEACH YOU IN SEX EDUCATION

We're not teachers (that's blatantly obvious, we know, and our hats go off to those classroom warriors), but coming up we have five important – nay, essential – points we would want to include if we were put in charge of a sex-ed class.

The entire concept of our sex education (we get it, it was a while ago...) was based on escaping sexually transmitted infections and avoiding pregnancy. Admittedly, we're well past our teens now, but the only thing we remember clearly from those painful 20-minute sessions taught by our form tutors is giggling, blushing and fumbling around with condoms and bananas or cucumbers.

If we were to revisit the Nineties and choose what we could learn about, we would cover the following five main points. We think that this information is vital to the wellbeing and health of teenagers and young adults as they navigate life, sex and fertility:

Getting pregnant isn't always easy

We do need to say here that while getting pregnant isn't always easy, one in three couples do get pregnant the first month of trying, so please don't make any changes to your birth control until you are actively trying to conceive. And STIs are still a big thing, so don't be silly, wrap that willy! But we should also be told that pregnancy might not be as simple as casting aside the condoms. According to the NHS website, around one in seven heterosexual couples will struggle to conceive (i.e. they will not become pregnant within a year of trying).

A positive pregnancy test does not always equate to a baby

When we get a positive pregnancy test, in our minds we've become a mum. We start planning the life that our baby will lead. We make a strong connection with the baby perceived to be growing inside us. However, with 25 per cent of pregnancies ending in loss (one in four pregnancies – repeat after us, one in four…), miscarriage and pregnancy loss are, sadly, realistic outcomes. So be armed with realistic expectations.

There is no such thing as normal (and the concept is highly overrated anyway)

Newsflash: not all cycles are twenty-eight days in length. Shocker, right?! During our school sex-ed lessons we learned that the female reproductive cycle is twenty-eight days long and that you lose about a spoonful of blood during a period (we don't know what spoon size they used for this, but during those heavy days, we were convinced it was towards the ladle end of the spoon spectrum). According to the NHS, anything from twenty-one days to forty days is 'normal' and **twenty-eight days is just an average**. And who wants to be average anyway?! If we were able to talk openly from a young age about our differences, without feeling ashamed, we could dispel any feelings of abnormality, and *actual* problems could be identified and treated.

Discharge is normal (and actually it can be your best mate)

Gross, right? Wrong! You ask any woman trying to have a baby how she feels about plentiful, slippery, transparent discharge and she'll tell you she bloody loves the stuff. The medical term is 'cervical mucus' (CM) (see page 256), which, yes, we admit sounds a bit gross, but it's mighty important. When you reach the point of ovulation (when an egg is released, ready to be fertilised) your CM will change from cloudy and white to slippery and transparent. CM is a sign that your bits and bobs are chugging away inside, and it only needs to be investigated if it starts to itch or smell funky.

All vulvas are different (and yours probably won't look like that of a porn star)

Porn is just – well, oh dear, where do we start? Porn creates unrealistic expectations of penises, vulvas, pleasure and body hair. Everyone's bits and bobs are different – from the size and shape to the smell and sensitivity. Some girls have large labia (lady-area lips) and some have barely any. Some girls have lots of pubic hair and some not so much. The fact of the matter is, everyone's lady gardens have the potential to give you pleasure. Exploring your body is key here, folks, and you can teach others to do the same (see Chapter 7).

*

See? Much better and much more informative. Begone, cucumbers and condoms! It's important to arm the younger generation with the power of knowledge and a recognition of the diversity of our bodies, and to teach them not to be scared of our differences. Let's give our future generations the respect they deserve and tell them how it really is. They can handle it.

DIFFERENT ROUTES TO PARENTING: SURROGACY

I (Laura) met Frances Simmons at a wedding (friend of a friend). I always knew her as a girl who used surrogacy, but I didn't know much else about her story until a few years later when she came on our podcast. As a teacher, Frances is passionate about dispelling the myths around pregnancy and arming teenagers with all the information. She co-hosts her own podcast about surrogacy, which is called *The Intended Parent*. It's a topic that no one talks about much and her podcast, which she hosts alongside Kreena Dhiman, another surrogacy mumma, is packed full of details and shares with listeners their unconventional journeys to motherhood.

FRANCES'S STORY

'If the only message girls hear at school is how to stop getting pregnant, then they are fooled into thinking it's going to be straightforward and easy when they do want a family.'

I am a science teacher and in Year Seven, when you are teaching reproduction, you have to do it in such a matter-of-fact way; 'If the sperm reaches the egg at this time in your menstrual cycle, then the egg fertilises, and you get pregnant.'

While you're at school a lot of the information you are given is from teachers. From my own point of view, I also got advice from my parents, which was all about how not to get pregnant. So, when you want to start a family, you think it will happen really quickly. I certainly thought that.

I think it's important to educate girls with both messages – you arm them with the knowledge that when they want to start a family, it might not necessarily be that easy. Because I think it's the expectation of something happening so easily when you want it to happen that is the hardest part of all. And then you are cross, and you think, 'Hang on, I have spent the past fifteen years thinking it will just happen and worrying unnecessarily.'

We had been trying for six months with no success when I found out I had cervical cancer. I was bleeding quite heavily after sex and then, because we hadn't got pregnant, I had a few tests and found out I had cancer and the best treatment involved me having a hysterectomy. It was a whirlwind of emotions. I felt like literally everything was happening so quickly. I was dealing with a cancer diagnosis and also the idea that I was never going to be able to carry a child myself.

I went into the world of IVF very blindly. It was our only option; we hadn't been researching it for years, and at the time my focus was on my cancer treatment. I went through IVF in a bit of a fog. A year later, we found an amazing lady who agreed to be our surrogate. As she already had three children, I thought to myself, 'OK, this will be easy,' but it took until the third round before we got a positive pregnancy test. I have now got two daughters and I think introducing different routes to parenting is what we should be educating young people about. And not just girls – educating boys too. It's a subject a lot of men clearly don't talk about with each other, so it's important to talk about those other routes and have an open dialogue about them.

There are still so many misconceptions out there about surrogacy too. My surrogate is one of the strongest women I know. She has found the whole process really empowering and there is no better example, I think, of women empowering women by doing this for each other. Perhaps it's something more women would do if they knew more about it.

I don't feel any less of a mum because I didn't carry the girls, and I know that in some ways having IVF and a surrogate as my only option was a good thing, because I never had the agony of thinking, 'Shall I keep trying if there is some small chance I might be able to carry my own child?' That wasn't a decision I had to make. And if we can tell young people about surrogacy and IVF and how different families are made, then we are arming them with knowledge – and that is only ever a good thing.

Frances Simmons (S2, E8)

LET'S TALK MORE ABOUT TALKING MORE

The first step, surely, in educating others is to talk more. Let's open up the dialogue surrounding miscarriage, infertility and baby loss and let's live in a world where no girl or woman should feel that any part of her body or its functionality should be kept a secret. Yes, we might sound like a Billy Big Bollocks, but if we can start the conversations and eliminate the misplaced shame that comes with anything that deviates from 'the norm', then our future generations can hit the ground running if problems arise. Because being 'normal' is ridiculously important to young girls, and feeling 'abnormal' is isolating and frightening.

It's likely that for many of us, the reality is that we can't ignore what has happened. We can't brush our experiences under the carpet because they live with us forever, so we must try to learn together how to expel the shame and ignite these conversations. We must support correctly – we must validate and we must acknowledge. This support can start here and now.

People don't know how to react when we lose our baby, so let's educate them. They want to make us feel better, but they don't know that isn't possible. We must be kind about that, because if we are angry and accuse them of not understanding, they will avoid the subject (and us) altogether.

Watching our dreams play out in the lives of others is painful. Watching others move on is So. Freaking. Hard. Knowing that the world keeps on spinning and other people keep doing their thing and living their lives while we stop and falter, unsure of which way to turn is such a painful place to be. So, when you are ready, and only then, please give your experience a voice. It's about sharing. Share your story and share your feelings. Tell your family and your friends what you need from them, gently. Tell them what you would find helpful; tell them what you don't find helpful (but acknowledge that you know it comes from a good place).

When one person who hasn't experienced baby loss is educated, they can pass it on, and this will create a new vibe around the subject. It will be a feeling of comfort and support rather than shame and isolation. Sharing your experience is empowering while identifying with the experience of others is liberating – let's make empowerment and liberation our gift to the women of the future. So get sharing – it starts right here, right now.

'When we share our stories, we are reminded of the humanity within each other. And when we take the time to understand each other's stories, we become more forgiving, more empathetic and more inclusive.'

MICHELLE OBAMA

HOW TO HELP OTHERS NAVIGATE YOUR GRIEF

It's not easy to articulate to friends and family how best to support you when you have experienced baby loss. Whether you are in the midst of grief or only just emerging from your trench, hearing the wrong thing or being told something in a blunt/brash/bitchy manner (however well meant, perhaps) might send you running back for cover. So let's work on how we can open eyes, ears and mouths to be more sensitive and supportive so that we are, ultimately, making the world a better place.

These little pointers might well be worth sharing with your family and friends who don't know what to say or do when they see you. It's a shitshow, we know, so point them in this direction.

1. **Check in (but don't expect too much):** This is a roller coaster for us and most of the time we won't know our arses from our elbows. Sometimes we will struggle to reply to a text, other times we will just want to vent and let it all out.

2. **Check in on our partners (but don't expect too much):** Make sure you call or text our partners if you can. Blokes especially will think that their grief is unjustified, as they haven't been through the loss physically. They won't want to burden us with their grief, but they will appreciate a message (see more on partner grief dos and don'ts on page 125).

3. **Never start a sentence with 'at least':** It doesn't matter how young we are, how early the loss was or if we already have a brood of healthy children. We are hurting and we need your love. You'll find more about the 'at leasts' in Chapter 3: Misconceptions (page 67).

4. **Don't be offended by our boundaries:** If we flake out last minute from social gatherings (especially baby-related ones), please don't be offended. We love you and we don't want to upset you, but we need to protect ourselves from any extra

heartbreak. We might unfollow social media accounts in the early days too, but that's our choice, so please don't question or judge us on these decisions.

5. **Be in the wings:** We know you are there if you send us a text – we might not reply, but by goodness, we know. And we won't forget that. When we are ready to be drawn out from our shells (don't try to pull us out too soon), we will let you know. And if you bring decent snacks, we will love you all the more.

6. **Offer practical support:** Don't just ask, 'Is there anything we can do?' Just DO it (sorry, Nike). Bring round cooked meals, organise a food shop, hang out the laundry or come round and walk the dogs for us. Actions will always speak louder than words.

7. **Remember to check in as the days turn to weeks and months:** We might look/behave like someone who is resilient, but the hours and seconds and days that pass don't make us stronger; we just get better at coping. We can't shower our babies with love, hold them to ease our pain, kiss them to release our sorrow, however much we so desperately want to. As the first few days and weeks of total devastation lessen their grip, we can also start to feel further away from our baby, and this can be frightening and send us spiralling.

8. **Be kind:** Returning to 'normal' life when we don't seem to fit in it anymore is a different challenge for us, and we still need care and attention. If you see us at work or on the school run with our other children, be kind. Always.

9. **Keep offering practical support:** As we begin to look like our old selves again, don't let us fool you. The surface is very different to what's happening inside, so continue to ask us how we feel – but *really* ask. Don't revert back to saying, 'Let me know if you need anything.' This just puts the onus on us

to ask for help and makes us feel like we are a burden. Doing the tiniest thing for us will be received with so much gratitude. Send a card, come over with a bottle of wine, buy a house plant... literally anything other than saying, 'Let me know if you need anything...'

10. **Remember special days/anniversaries/birthdays:** These will be especially hard for us. Keep offering practical support. Keep being kind. We've found such love and validation when other people remember those dates. It's acknowledgement that our baby existed in this world, not just in our hearts and bodies. Say their names, talk about the pregnancy, don't be worried about reminding or upsetting us – our babies are constantly on our minds and the acknowledgement of their existence far outweighs the pang of sadness.

NB: And number 11... (which is more than a point, so deserves its own NB). It's human nature to try to say something to make someone feel better. But actually, just sitting with someone in their grief is worth a hundred well-intended words. Sit with us, hold us, cry with us too. If you get the emotions associated with what we are going through, that's our baby sending shockwaves and leaving their legacy with that raw emotion. An 'I'm sorry, it's shit, I'm here for you' is worth a million 'At least it was early's'.

DIFFERENT ROUTES TO PARENTING: ADOPTION

Not a Fictional Mum, or 'Nota' as we endearingly call her (the nickname Bex gave her), is another absolute powerhouse who acts as a voice, campaigner and advocate for adopters and adoptees – a path to parenthood that she came to following her own baby-loss experience. Check out her website for more details of some of her campaigns.

NOT A FICTIONAL MUM'S STORY

'It's not just about educating pupils about different routes they might have to parenthood, but also recognising that you have children sat in your classroom that have come into their families in a different way.'

After trying to conceive naturally for a long time, we went for some tests and were basically told that it wasn't going to happen without medical intervention. I choose not to publicly share the whos or whys of the medical diagnosis because we already live in a society where people become obsessed with knowing which partner has the problem. If two people are in love and want to have a child together but one of them can't, then they both have the issue.

We were offered one free cycle of IVF on the NHS and, when that didn't work, we started paying. We invested in more cycles, which came at a huge financial cost. We did get pregnant but devastatingly lost our pregnancy. Still, we decided to have another shot before thinking, 'This is insanity.' It was having a huge impact on us as individuals – psychologically, emotionally, financially.

We had conversations prior to looking at adoption about what made a family and we both agreed that for us it was about having a child that we could love, support and influence as they grew. When we started to think about the genetic aspect of starting a family and we realised that it wasn't important for us, it was the start of us exploring adoption.

But we did have to grieve first. We had to take time to grieve for the life we'd assumed we would have. It's really important to take that time. You won't see your partner in your child; your genetic story is ending and that's a huge thing to get your head around. There is a total misconception that people have when you can't have children naturally, which goes along the lines of, 'Oh, you can always just adopt.' That's a dangerous mindset to have, as adopting a child will not replace the loss of a biological child. An adopted child is not a replacement for what didn't happen for you. It's a very unhealthy way of thinking and for our children to be thought of – that they are just a replacement. An adopted child is their own person; a human being who has their own life history and their own genetics, and if you do embark on the adoption process, you will understand that it is an entirely different route into parenthood altogether. It's non-comparable to having a child biologically.

At no point when we went to see doctors about not being able to conceive naturally was adoption mentioned to us. There was every other route under the sun, but never adoption. So at what point should we introduce adoption as a route to parenthood?

When I think back to when I was at school, there would have been one or two children who would have been adopted – statistically speaking, there must have been – and there would have been children born through surrogates or IVF, but their routes to their families were never mentioned. And that makes me so sad – it's not only about educating children about different routes to parenthood, but also recognising that you have children sat in your classroom who have come into their families in a different way.

We have an unspeakably beautiful relationship with our son. I knew I would love him, and I knew I would think he was gorgeous and all the things you do think with children, but I wasn't prepared to respect him in the way that I do because he is just remarkable. There is another huge misconception too, where I have had people say to me, 'Oh, everything's fine now you've adopted.' Of course, we are very happy, but we can't forget the trauma we went through to get to him – and all the trauma he had to get to us. We can't pretend it didn't happen, but we accept it, and we pull each other through it.

Not a Fictional Mum (S4, E6), www.notafictionalmum.com

THE LOST BABIES... THE SISTERS AND THE BROTHERS

While schools don't teach much around miscarriage and baby loss in sex-ed classes, there are a huge number of pupils who will have experienced both situations indirectly. We are talking about the sons and daughters – the ones who see their mum in tears every morning; the brothers and sisters who won't ever get to cuddle their new siblings. What are we doing to support these children?

It's devastating for the WHOLE family when baby loss occurs – and children aren't stupid. They know how babies are made because age-appropriate lessons are taught. But they sure as hell don't understand why babies are lost. Let's support them. Let's show them we care.

Depending on when baby loss occurred, your child might have seen your pregnancy bump grow. They might have seen you buy baby products, or they might even have come with you to a scan. Here are a few things that we could keep in mind when it comes to educating children about lost brothers and sisters:

Reassure them first that you are OK. This is likely to be their biggest worry.

Reassure them that no one is to blame for what has happened. When bad things happen, children often want a person to blame or to hate for a while.

Reassure them that it's definitely not their fault. If they are older and perhaps had an argument with you about staying out too late or not picking up their dirty towels from the floor, they might instinctively think they are to blame because they upset you or caused you stress. You will need to make this abundantly clear: no one did anything wrong.

Reassure them that you are sad so they, too, can process the sadness and not try to protect you. Teenagers might think that they should try to be happy around you and not be upset in case it makes you sad. By being open about our emotions and sadness, we are encouraging them by example to share how they feel with us, as we are sharing with them.

Children pick up on our emotions because they are so intuitive. Which means younger children, who might not understand what miscarriage is or that there might have been another baby to share Mummy with, will certainly feel upset if they see you upset.

The Miscarriage Association (www.miscarriageassociation.org.uk) encourages using an analogy for the process of 'miscarriage' when explaining it to children. For example, describing pregnancy as being like planting seeds in a garden, only some seeds don't grow into full plants.

In times of grief, a family can come together in ways that no one anticipates. The teens that have previously been glued to computer screens might feel just being around you a comfort. Regardless of your children's age, planning a family activity that marks the loss in some way – planting a tree, taking a trip to the beach (there is literally no way that being blown away by a sea breeze or feeling the sand between your toes might not, however momentarily, boost the mood of your whole party) or agreeing to spend an evening all together on a regular basis – might benefit everyone.

If you're finding the explanation of baby loss and miscarriage challenging because your children are too young to fully 'get it' but old enough to know something has happened, there are lots of picture books aimed at younger children which can help explain (see the Resources section on page 275 for some ideas). And children do love asking a question (or several thousand), so this might be a good place to start.

'If Mum ain't happy, ain't no one happy!' or so goes that old chestnut. But of course, there is a great deal of truth to this. Parents set the mood for families, and while we try to do everything possible to protect our children from bad news or feeling sad, we might be unintentionally isolating them. Grieving in children can look very different to grieving in adults, so let's make sure we all have the time and space to support and help each other.

If an older child is finding it especially tough but feels that they will only be adding to your upset by talking about it, encourage them to speak to a close friend or family member who not only completely gets the situation, but gets them. Grandmothers are good for this. They often don't need to be told what the problem is when a grandchild comes knocking, and a hot chocolate, a plate of digestives and a change of scene can work wonders for a confused and emotional child. We speak from experience here: in these situations, grannies/grandmas/nanas/nannies/g-mas are worth their weight in gold.

'We want to tell you something, so there won't be any doubt.
You are so wonderful to think of, but so hard to be without.'

PARTNER CHECK-IN

Our partners deserve a special box of love and attention because although they might not experience the same physical loss that we do, they will still feel the emotional impact, and this should be understood. We all grieve in different ways, and often with this very specific kind of grief the focus is all on the partner who has experienced the physical loss. So please signpost friends and family to these little nuggets below to help them communicate with and support your partner:

DO ask about them in a way that is just about them and not the rest of the family, so that they know they are cared about as much as everyone else. Single them out with a message, a call, a knock on the door.

DO tell them their feelings are valid in whatever guise they take – guilt, anger, blame, frustration. There is no judgement here. It's all normal and a healthy part of grief.

DO be practical. Perhaps they won't want to sit down and talk about how they are feeling, but suggesting a bike ride, dog walk, jog together can give them the space and opportunity to open up.

DON'T simply assume they are only worth a brief note of consideration. Partners need to be asked how they are doing, how they are feeling, how they are coping too – and on a regular basis. Not only will they have their own emotions surrounding the loss, but often they feel they must be 'strong' for their partner and so don't talk to them for fear of burdening an already broken heart.

DON'T tell them it will soon get easier. Grief isn't linear. It might ease in the long run, but you mustn't set them up with false expectations that their feelings will quickly disappear over the coming weeks.

DON'T tell them they are grieving in a specific way. If you put a label on their grief – 'you are grieving like a man', for example – you will make them feel that they can't cry when the anger subsides because that isn't 'the normal way for a man to grieve'.

THE VILLAGE OPENED ITS ARMS

'My friend made a WhatsApp group without me in it with my close family and friends. They organised all these things, practical things – like a rota for dropping off meals or care packages – during a time when I couldn't face constant calls or a thousand well-meaning messages. Then, after a while, I could join in the communication of what I needed, too.'

TAHNEE KNOWLES, THE MINDFUL GRIEF COACH

Remember the old chestnut 'It takes a village to raise a child'? Well, that village is there for you when you have empty arms too. Reach out to your village. In the early days of grief, know your village is there for you even if you want to hide away from them. Let the force of the village come through in just one or two people – a friend or a family member. Pick out a couple of people who have shown they have the emotional intelligence to get what you need and ask them to be your go-tos for the rest of the family or your friends. It can be exhausting to try to speak to everyone, to form words that make any sense, to even make a noise… and that's OK.

Chapter 10

Power in the Tribe

'We often form stronger bonds with those who recognise our suffering.'

HEALING LIES IN SHARING AND KINDNESS

When you lose a baby, it can feel as though you lose your place in society. You are no longer an expectant mother and you're not a new mum, but you feel very far from the care-free romance of trying to conceive for the first time. It's difficult to know where you are, and it seems like others struggle to find you a place within their worlds as well. Are you infertile, or are you not? You feel as though you don't belong anywhere, and that is hugely isolating and frightening.

When we started *TWGGE*, our aim was to share our pain in the hope that we could help just one woman feel less alone. We found that writing and talking about grief not only resonated with more of you than we could have imagined. It also aided our own personal ongoing healing process. So, we wanted to say a big thank you to every one of you for offering so much love and support to us and each other.

Our stories, no matter what they are, empower us as women, but we know that not everyone is keen on sharing. Many of us stood and watched this community from the sidelines for a little while before getting involved, and that's totally OK. Broken people save broken people, and together we are stronger. We are pack animals, aren't we? People love being part of something and *TWGGE* is a community that you can cling to. We want to give women a platform and a place to feel that they belong.

We need a new narrative for baby loss and miscarriage. As a society, the way we are looking at the subject still leads us to believe we are abnormal. Yes, baby loss is devastating, but part of the devastation is that it is so common and yet so rarely discussed. The subject is still shrouded in mystery and misplaced shame, and all the time we are not talking about it, we are feeding into the idea that it *should* be kept private. The problem is systemic and must be confronted in order for us to help future generations navigate and manage the totally unique grief and pain of baby loss without the isolation and loneliness that still accompanies the experience now. Miscarriage and baby loss are not abnormal at all! They're f**king awful but sadly not abnormal. It's just not talked about and all that does is fuel the mystery and the stigma behind it.

We hope that after reading this book, you will realise just how far you are from being alone. There are thousands of warriors out there and we have spoken to a mere handful. Talking of warriors, we have saved Clair Alleebux's story for this chapter because, well, it covers all aspects of this book and epitomises the *TWGGE* spirit. Clair's story could very easily have sat among any of our chapters, but it rounds off the book in a way that perhaps nothing we can say really will. Clair's loss probably came much later than that of most of you reading this book; however, the difficulties and emotions are relatable to anyone dealing with baby loss. The legacy she has created and the money she has raised for the charity Children With Cancer is phenomenal.

CLAIR'S STORY

'As much as you hear about bad people in the world, there are also lots of lovely, caring people in the world, and when they reach out to you when you are going through such an awful time, it's so appreciated.'

You think getting pregnant will be straightforward, and you start thinking something is wrong when it doesn't happen straight away, don't you? In reality, the average time it takes is a year. So, hearing that we fell into the 'norm' bracket was reassuring, and we tried not to focus on it so much. I was fit and healthy and when I did fall pregnant, I went into it quite confidently. I felt very healthy throughout. I didn't even get much morning sickness, and I have such fond memories of my labour, nearly giving birth at home by the front door!

Our son, Lucas, was born on 21 September and, from that day, we were a family of three. We settled into life at home. We were very proud parents – we'd go for little walks with him and it was just perfect. When I was changing him one morning when he was about three weeks old, I noticed his facial expressions didn't seem right. He was crying and I wasn't sure quite what was wrong. I was a new mum and part of me thought, 'Is it me? Am I looking for something that isn't there?' But then my husband came into the room and immediately said, 'Does his face look a bit strange to you?' One side of his face wasn't moving when he was crying, so we got him dressed and took him to the hospital and a paediatrician spotted the facial palsy straight away. She told us that in all her sixteen years working she hadn't seen a facial palsy in a baby this young and so she arranged an emergency MRI scan.

We had the weekend to wait and as we walked to the hospital on Monday, I said to Lucas, 'This is a big day for you, little man,' and I wanted everything to be fine. We went in and had the MRI and while we were in the waiting room waiting for the results, two of my friends, who were also pregnant and due around the same time, messaged me to say they had had their babies and had both had boys too. I remember thinking, 'I hope all our boys will be able to play with each other as they get older.' Then we got called into a room and as soon as we went in, we immediately picked up that something wasn't right. They had found a brain tumour on Lucas's scan.

Suddenly everything was a blur. A taxi had been arranged to take us straight to Great Ormond Street Hospital (GOSH), where a radiologist had already been briefed. It all happened so quickly – we were shipped off and met by the radiologist, who outlined a plan for that week. Our precious baby needed a specific MRI to have a closer look at the tumour, and an ultrasound to look at his organs, and they wanted to do a biopsy and make an incision into his brain to try to debulk as much of the tumour as they could.

Lucas was in theatre for nearly seven hours. I cried as I handed him over and he was sent to sleep – I couldn't get over the image of them trying to get to this tumour in his tiny head. Afterwards they told us they weren't able to debulk the tumour as much as they wanted because of where it was in the brain. They called us into a room and asked a nurse to watch Lucas while they outlined the situation.

Lucas was four weeks old, with an aggressive tumour. They grow quite rapidly, and they just said, 'If we try to treat this tumour, the outcome will be the same. There are very few survivors of this type of tumour – we would just be prolonging his life.'

We were given the option of taking Lucas to the local hospice, local hospital or home, and my husband immediately said, 'I want to take him home.' I was so afraid because what did that mean? Taking him home to die, that's what it meant. A few months ago, we were overjoyed that our first child was on the way and now we were taking our baby home to die. When we walked through the door, the first thing I saw were all my congratulations cards and I just said, 'Take them down, take them all down!'

We had so much support from friends and family, who didn't overcrowd us and gave us our own space to let us be together as a family. We had nurses, community nurses and palliative nurses from GOSH and they talked us through the end-of-life care plan. The brain tumour was shutting down Lucas's organs and he couldn't see and couldn't hear and couldn't feed. You see it take hold before your eyes and it feels like you are living in a nightmare. You want it to end for everyone – and that's a horrible thing to say, as you want to be with your baby forever, but it's so unbearable watching them go through so much pain.

Lucas was unconscious a lot of the time and changing your baby when he's like that is hard – it feels like you are changing a lifeless baby. The day he passed away, he hadn't fed all night, even through the gastric tube – his body was rejecting the food and it was coming out and it wasn't nice at all. He was quite blue, and I phoned the nurses quite early and I said, 'I think he's ready to go today.'

We sat with Lucas and I thought it would be quite quick but

it went on for hours. The tumour suffocates them, so they look like they are being strangled and their face starts distorting. It would come in waves and it was horrible. The nurses explained that it was just his body shutting down. We knew Lucas wasn't in discomfort, but it was almost unbearably hard to watch.

My husband said I had to hold him – 'You are his mummy, you have to hold him' – and in the end, it was seven weeks to the day, to the hour – nearly to the minute – after he was born that he passed away. He looked so peaceful; he looked like an angel. I couldn't speak. I wasn't crying, I wasn't screaming, it was just an uncontrollable wailing. It felt like someone had literally put their hand in my chest and pulled my heart out.

It was so hard for me to see my husband in so much pain when Lucas died; it was awful. People have asked us so many times about how we got through it as a couple, but it was simple for us – we had to for Lucas. We were on round-the-clock care for Lucas at home, so we needed to be on the ball. We had to make sure we were constantly communicating and working as a team, and we needed to be there for each other. And we felt so overwhelmed with the kindness and support we received from so many people. When you are going through such a challenging time, just knowing that your family and friends are all there meant so much. We would have food shops dropped off, messages from people that said, 'Don't even think about responding' – just messages to show they were there.

As much as you hear about bad people in the world, there are also lots of lovely, caring people, and when they reach out to you when you are going through such an awful time, it's so appreciated. We have friends who still send cards on Lucas's birthday and that means so much, that really does – that people acknowledge his birthday.

We spoke to our doctor a while after Lucas died, and he said to us, 'I suppose one of the things you are talking about is having another baby. It's OK to want another baby,' he said. 'You had Lucas because as a couple you wanted to start a family, and that hasn't gone away. Don't feel guilty.' And hearing that from a professional felt like we had permission; it felt like we weren't being judged.

It was a very bizarre feeling when I fell pregnant again with my son Joel and people would ask, 'Oh, is this your first pregnancy?' And I would always reply, 'No, no, it's not.' I would never want to deny Lucas. When I meet other parents who have lost babies, the first thing I say to them is not to think that having another baby makes everything better or makes everything go away. It doesn't; it brings about a whole other set of emotions to get your head round. You are still grieving and yet you are worried about this pregnancy. Then you feel guilty because you aren't happy about this pregnancy, because you want to be happy, but you are scared.

I have three children: I have Lucas and his legacy, and I have a son called Joel and a daughter called Margot. And we talk about Lucas all the time. We take the kids to Lucas's grave, which is in a woodland area and there are lots of other babies buried beneath some beautiful oak trees, so I know he isn't alone. We take birthday cake when it's his birthday because he is part of me and part of our family. He might not be here, but he has a presence, always.

Clair Alleebux MBE (S1, E14 & 15)

You can find Clair's fundraising website in memory of Lucas on page 277.

When we started *The Worst Girl Gang Ever* during lockdown in 2020, we did it to help just one person feel less alone. Never in a million years could we have imagined we'd be leading this epic community and supporting warriors from all around the globe. Our heartfelt thanks go out to each and every one of you. We are incredibly proud of this community and despite it being the 'worst' girl gang ever, it is full of the most incredible women – women who have supported and empowered us on our own personal journeys.

Remember, you're not all in the same boat, but you are all in the storm and we've got you. Because we're a mother-f**king lighthouse. And we say, let's get talking. Let's get sharing. Let's get supporting and let's get empowering. No more shame, no more taboo. Let's ditch that for the sake of our children – the ones who are, the ones who will come, and in memory of the ones who never came to be.

Medical Glossary

Medical terminology is thrown around, and sometimes, when you suddenly find yourself in the baby-loss community, you quickly start throwing it around too. But believe us when we say, there is nothing more intimidating when you've just gone through this horrendous experience than realising you don't understand anything that anyone is saying to you.

Medical terms don't carry any emotion. They are stark and scary and seem to want to make everything black and white and 'official'. That's just the way of the medical profession; that's the way they deal with it. It's a way of labelling your experience using neatly defined jargon.

Well, you know what? We are more than these labels. Medical words come with connotations and emotions and implications attached. So, in this section, we are aiming to include all the official terms that might be relevant to baby loss and break them down. Don't be afraid to mess with the jargon either – use it, personalise it, preach it and don't let the words feel scary or frightening.

We've taken all the following facts and information from the NHS and Tommy's websites, which provide far more guidance than we can cover here (all of it is current and up to date at time of publication, but science and medicine are bloody wonderful, and things are changing all the time, so be sure to do your own research). The awkward jokes, the swearing and the other waffle is all us. You're welcome.

A–Z OF MEDICAL TERMS

ASHERMAN'S SYNDROME

Otherwise known as intrauterine adhesions/scarring or synechiae, this is a uterine condition where scarring (or adhesions) occurs inside the uterus and/or cervix. Often the back walls of the uterus stick together, but in less severe cases the scarring only occurs in a small part of the ute. These adhesions can be thick or thin, dotted about, in one location or joined together.

Symptoms can include:

- irregular or non-existent periods.
- period pain but no bleed, which indicates that menstruation is occurring, but blood can't exit the uterus because the adhesions have blocked the exit to the cervix.
- recurrent miscarriage and/or infertility.

The main causes of AS (in over 90 per cent of cases) are pregnancy-related D&C's (Dilation and Curettage procedure, minor surgery where the cervix is dilated and a doctor uses a curette to remove tissue from inner lining of your uterus) or a retained placenta following delivery. Any trauma to the ute lining triggers a normal wound-healing process, which can cause the damaged areas to fuse together. It can affect fertility because the adhesions affect the blood supply to the uterus, meaning a fertilised egg can't implant in the lining. The adhesions can also act as a physical barrier for sperm. Removal of the scar tissue via hysteroscopy is the treatment.

BABY LOSS AWARENESS WEEK (BLAW)

Not a medical term or one that needs explaining, but we wanted to highlight this annual awareness week in October because we reckon each year will bring more education, more sharing and more empowerment, which can only ever be a good thing.

IMPORTANT: This is an emotional and exhausting week for many, and you should not feel pressured into doing anything or saying anything if you are finding things tough. This is OK. We can't be warriors every day. Just promise us that you will do what you need to do to get through it and know that we've got you.

BLIGHTED OVUM (BO)

Sometimes referred to as anembryonic pregnancy/embryonic loss or an embryonic demise (because why have one phrase when you can have several?!), blighted ovum describes a particular type of early miscarriage.

A BO occurs when the cells of a baby stop developing early on, and the tiny embryo is reabsorbed. However, the pregnancy sac, where the baby should develop, continues to grow. It's thought that a BO pregnancy happens due to a chromosomal abnormality in the egg.

It can be diagnosed at an ultrasound scan, which might show a sac with no developing baby inside. Sometimes this is described as 'showing no foetal pole'. So, the crap bits:

- A BO is often discovered between eight and twelve weeks of pregnancy at a routine scan.
- Hormone levels are still high, giving a positive pregnancy test and pregnancy symptoms.

- When the pregnancy hormones subside, a miscarriage should happen naturally. You might be offered medication or surgery to speed up the process, in which case you might have to wait a week or two for a second scan to confirm diagnosis.

Now, the important bit… your baby existed the moment you discovered you were pregnant. No one can take them from you, no matter the diagnosis. A shit-ton of love to you.

CERVICAL MUCUS (CM)

There is no such thing as TMI with us because no woman should feel embarrassed or ashamed of what their bodies produce. And cervical mucus is a very normal and natural part of your menstrual cycle.

- CM is a fluid that is secreted by the cervix, which helps to keep the vagina healthy, protecting against infection and providing lubrication.
- The consistency, colour and amount of CM can change throughout your menstrual cycle and if you monitor your CM, it will help identify your fertile days.
- When you are at your most fertile you will notice an increase in CM; it will be wetter and more slippery, and it looks and feels like raw egg whites, stretching to about 5cm without breaking in the middle (see, there is no such thing as TMI).
- This egg-white cervical mucus shows you're at your most fertile and the best chance of conceiving is to have sex every two or three days during this fertile time.

How to check: Wipe with clean toilet paper or insert a clean finger into your vagina, reaching up towards your cervix.

How not to check: When camping, especially if you leave the tent window/door unzipped. For more on this tale, listen to S1, E12 of the podcast.

CHEMICAL PREGNANCY (CP)

Defined by Tommy's as a very early pregnancy loss. It is diagnosed when a pregnancy is confirmed by a blood test or home pregnancy test but can't be seen on an ultrasound can, usually up until around five weeks of pregnancy. Symptoms of a chemical pregnancy can include:

- a positive pregnancy test followed by a negative one.
- mild spotting before your period is due.
- mild abdominal cramping.
- vaginal bleeding following a positive test.
- Low HCG levels in the blood (this is the hormone produced by the placenta when pregnant).

The most common cause of a chemical pregnancy is thought to be a chromosomal problem with the developing baby and usually doesn't require any medical intervention or treatment. You might notice that your period is heavier or more painful than normal and you may pass some small blood clots. Right, that is the bluntness. Now the reality. The shitty shittiness of a CP is that while it's an 'early' miscarriage in a purely medical sense, as soon as you see those two blue lines you begin to dream about a future that, unbeknown to you, will never exist. Even if you only knew you were pregnant for a few days, it is OK to grieve. It's valid and you are not alone.

CHROMOSOMES

Unless you paid particular attention in biology class, you probably won't be hearing much about these rod-shaped structures until you start thinking about the sort of characteristics you want in a partner so you can pass on all the attractive genes to your baby. Chromosomes carry the genes, and these genes decide the sex of the baby and the characteristics it will inherit from its parents. Sadly, in the *TWGGE* world, we tend to hear about chromosomal abnormalities, which happen if a baby carries too many or not enough chromosomes. A human body cell usually contains forty-six chromosomes arranged in twenty-three pairs (twenty-three from the mother and twenty-three from the father), but when an abnormality occurs, the baby won't be able to develop properly.

EARLY PREGNANCY UNIT (EPU)

The EPU is where you are likely to be referred if you are in the early stages of pregnancy and there are some concerns – the most common reasons being that you might be bleeding and/or have pain after a positive pregnancy test.

It's likely you will be between five and fourteen weeks pregnant when under the care of the EPU, whose work centres around ultrasounds to confirm the location and viability of your pregnancy. You might also be referred if you have a previous history of problems in early pregnancy, such as *Recurrent miscarriages* (see page 268), *Molar pregnancy* (see page 264) or an *Ectopic pregnancy* (see next page).

It's a place no one wants to go. The anxiety and panic hangs heavy in the air, but we want you to know that the nurses who work here know that emotions will be high and the shit-show is real. We've got you. (See also, *Transvaginal ultrasound scan* – or a Wanda/probe/lightsaber up your foofie – page 272.)

ECTOPIC PREGNANCY (EP)

An EP is when a fertilised egg implants itself outside of the womb, usually in one of the fallopian tubes. If an egg does get stuck there, it won't develop and it won't be possible to save the pregnancy. According to the NHS website, around one in every 90 pregnancies is ectopic.

An EP doesn't always cause symptoms and might only be detected during a routine scan. However, you might experience some of the following symptoms:

- a missed period (or other signs of pregnancy).
- tummy pain low down on one side.
- brown, watery discharge or vaginal bleeding.
- discomfort when you use the toilet.
- Shoulder tip pain, although uncommon, is an unusual pain felt where your shoulder ends and your arm begins. You should get medical advice right away if you experience this.

These symptoms are not exclusive to an EP, but if they become more severe (including sudden, sharp and intense pain in your tummy, feeling sick or very dizzy, or suddenly becoming very pale) you should immediately seek advice from your midwife or GP or go straight to A&E. These severe signs can happen in a few cases when an EP can grow large enough to split open the fallopian tube (known as a rupture) which is extremely serious.

If an EP is detected at a routine scan, you will be advised of three main treatments available:

- Expectant management: you will be carefully monitored and if the fertilised egg doesn't dissolve by itself, you will be offered one of the following treatments:

- Medication: an injection of methotrexate to stop the pregnancy progressing.
- Surgery: a laparoscopy (keyhole surgery) is performed to remove the fertilised egg along with the affected fallopian tube.

Having an EP is devastating. Not only do we feel utterly robbed by the fact that it was a viable pregnancy (fertilised egg) which just decided to bed down in the wrong place, but there is such a short window between diagnosis and treatment (to ensure no further, more serious problems to the woman develop) that we often feel overwhelmed and in shock due to the speed of management. And that's before you digest the idea that you might have to go through emergency surgery due to very serious, life-risking complications. Give yourself time afterwards to grieve. Be gentle with yourself. We know you will want to make sense of it, but there is no blame and no fault to be found within you. Giving you lots of *TWGGE* love and support.

ENDOMETRIOSIS

A long-term condition where tissue, similar to the lining of the womb, grows in other places. This can include the ovaries and fallopian tubes. Symptoms can include:

- severe period pains.
- lower back pain.
- pain during and after sex.
- difficulty getting pregnant.
- pain when going to the toilet.

Treatment can vary depending on severity but can include:

- Hormone medicines and contraceptives are used to treat women with mild symptoms. The hormones in the contraceptive pill cause the uterus lining to become thinner, causing periods to be shorter and lighter and thus reducing symptoms.
- Surgery: this aims to remove the deposits of endometriosis, therefore reducing the pain caused.
- Hysterectomy: there is currently no definitive cure for endometriosis. Removing the uterus and ovaries is the most effective treatment. However, there is no guarantee that the symptoms will never return.

According to Tommy's, around seven in ten women with mild to moderate endometriosis conceive without treatment, but if you have any concerns or symptoms, go and see your GP. Be persistent with this one, as we have heard from many women who have waited far too long for a diagnosis.

INCOMPETENT CERVIX

What a shit name. Any term that feels like it lays the blame at the feet of the pregnancy-loss sufferer is a crock of shit. No one is diagnosed with incompetent ears if they are deaf. Because it's not your fault, ever. BUT we also get that for some women, this might be a comfort. To know that there is nothing you could have done, or that however hard you tried, your cervix couldn't quite handle a pregnancy, might take away some of the guilt. We just feel defensive about this one because we struggle with the word 'incompetent'. It seems so insensitive, so unkind. OK, rant over…

An incompetent cervix (sometimes called cervical insufficiency) is when the cervix shortens and opens in the second trimester or early in the third trimester without any other symptoms of labour, which can cause premature birth or the loss of an otherwise healthy pregnancy.

The most common treatment is a cerclage or a stitch, a strong suture in and around the cervix between twelve and fourteen weeks. It prevents the spontaneous opening and is removed at the end of pregnancy when risk of miscarriage is low. Management includes:

- *Transvaginal ultrasound scan* (see page 272) for monitoring (also known as Wanda/the lightsaber).
- vaginal swabs to check for the substance that is present when you are at increased risk of going into labour.
- antibiotic treatment to try to reduce the risk of infection
- *Progesterone pessaries* (see page 267), also known as 'bum wax', to 'harden the cervix'.

LOW-DOSE ASPIRIN (LDA)

Aspirin isn't exactly a WTAF word, but chances are you will come across it used and discussed at certain points in the context of pregnancy loss, so it's always worth unpacking it.

Aspirin is a blood-thinning medication and is known as a NSAID (a non-steroidal anti-inflammatory drug), which we know is often used to treat pain, fever or inflammation. Sometimes we see LDA (which can also be known as baby aspirin) as a recurring theme on miscarriage forums or support groups and this is because (thank you, NHS website) one of the causes of *Recurrent miscarriage* (see page 268) is thought to be antiphospholipid syndrome (APS), which can sometimes be called Hughes syndrome or sticky blood.

So, what the actual is APS/Hughes syndrome/sticky blood?

- This is a disorder of the immune system that causes an increased risk of blood clots.
- It's treated during pregnancy with low-dose aspirin and heparin. Aspirin is an antiplatelet medication, which means it interrupts the process of blood-clot formation so they don't form where they are not needed.
- Heparin is an anticoagulation medication and is used to decrease the clotting ability of the blood.
- To diagnose APS, the blood needs to be tested for the abnormal antiphospholipid antibodies that increase the risk of blood clots and you will need to ask your GP for the test. While LDA is often prescribed during pregnancy, always check with your midwife or GP before you start taking it.

MISSED MISCARRIAGE (MMC) OR SILENT MISCARRIAGE

This is a miscarriage with absolutely no symptoms, no pain and no bleeding. It happens to one in thirty women, so this isn't the stuff of urban myth and shouldn't be 'silent', as there is something brutal in the reality.

An MMC can leave you feeling like you have been cruelly tricked by your own body, because it doesn't usually carry any obvious symptoms. And it F**KING sucks. The NHS reports that most miscarriages happen due to a chromosomal abnormality and an MMC is no different. But the big difference is that when an MMC happens hormone levels don't drop immediately after the baby dies. Your body still believes you are pregnant.

You are usually given three options at this point:

- Medical management: a drug can be taken orally or vaginally to induce the miscarriage.

263

- Surgical management: under a general anaesthetic, the contents of the uterus are removed vaginally with suction.
- Natural management: no intervention is taken, and you wait for nature to take its course.

Our hearts go out to anyone who has been blindsided by MMC. It really is horrific and there are no words… Just remember that you are a warrior and that talking about, writing about or sharing your experiences will give others strength. Take it one day at a time.

MOLAR PREGNANCY (MP)

An MP is caused by a problem with the fertilised egg at the point of conception. It means that the baby and placenta do not develop the way they should and the pregnancy will not be able to survive. According to Tommy's website, it affects one in every 600 pregnancies. MP is recognised on an ultrasound scan between eight and fourteen weeks but won't be confirmed until further tests are carried out. There are two types:

- Complete molar: a single sperm fertilises an 'empty' egg. A foetus doesn't develop.
- Partial molar: two sperm fertilise an egg, so there might be some early signs of a foetus, but the baby will not develop far enough to be able to survive outside of the uterus.

The pregnancy can end with its own miscarriage, but, more usually, a surgical procedure is required to remove all the pregnancy tissue. This is important because the cells continue to grow, so blood and urine hormone levels will be monitored regularly until they reach zero. You will be grieving not only for your loss, but for the opportunity to soon try again as this process can take months. There's lots and lots to say on this, so please visit the NHS, the Miscarriage Association and Tommy's websites if you need more information.

NATURAL KILLER (NK) CELLS

NK cells form part of the body's immune system, and they help the body fight infection and cancer. Every organ has NK cells to protect it, including the uterus. In the uterus they are called uNK cells and they play an important role in getting pregnant because they help the wall of the womb inflame slightly so the embryo can implant into the uterine wall.

Too many or too few uNK cells, however, can either cause too much or too little inflammation, both of which are associated with infertility and miscarriage.

Running a test to find out your NK situ isn't routinely done on the NHS, although some fertility clinics do offer it. If you are diagnosed as having an abnormal uNK cell count, treatment is aimed at suppressing the number and the activity of those cells, and includes medication such as prednisolone, which is a steroid commonly used for asthma and arthritis.

POLYCYSTIC OVARY SYNDROME (PCOS)

This is a condition related to hormones in which the ovaries don't always release an egg at the end of the menstrual cycle. It is thought this condition affects one in every ten women in the UK (did ANYONE know this?!) and if you have polycystic ovaries (PCO) they will be slightly larger than 'normal' and you will have many more follicles (the fluid-filled pockets on the ovaries that release the eggs when you ovulate). BUT – and this is a biggie – having a PCO doesn't mean you have PCOS. This is a disorder that is linked to a hormone imbalance. The exact cause is unknown, but it may be genetic because you're more likely to have it if your mothers, aunts, sisters, etc., have it. Another good reason to get all this shizzle out in the open.

Symptoms of PCOS include:

- irregular or no periods.
- more facial or body hair.
- less hair on the head.
- difficulty losing weight or rapid weight gain.
- acne or oily skin.
- difficulty in becoming pregnant.

A diagnosis of PCOS is made when you have any two of the following symptoms, in which case go and see your GP and get a referral to a gynaecologist:

- irregular or no periods.
- a transvaginal scan showing polycystic ovaries.
- an increase in facial or body hair or test results showing an excess in testosterone.

POST-TRAUMATIC STRESS DISORDER (PTSD)

You might be thinking that you have only heard of this disorder being linked with soldiers and war and stuff (and we were the same), but PTSD can occur when you experience any traumatic event – one that provokes fear, helplessness or horror in response to the threat of injury or death. Miscarriage is a traumatic event.

The symptoms of PTSD are split into four categories:

- Re-experiencing: for example, nightmares or flashbacks.
- Avoidance: staying away from people or places; drug and/or alcohol misuse; feeling numb.
- Reactivity: feeling tense or jumpy, or having angry outbursts.
- Cognition and mood: feeling overwhelming negative emotions like sadness, fear, guilt, shame and a loss of trust in people.

If you have experienced some or all of these symptoms following baby loss, we want to reassure you that, while this is brutal, it is very ordinary. Make sure you seek help from your GP and explain why you think you might have PTSD. There is so much help and advice out there for you or your partner (partners can also get PTSD following miscarriage), and your GP will be able to get you the help you need. You are not alone.

PROGESTERONE PESSARY

We like to call things as we see them, and one of our deliciously cheeky (wait for it) warriors has coined the phrase 'bum wax' for this term. It is, in essence, a candle up the bum.

The progesterone hormone prepares the uterus for pregnancy after ovulation by triggering the lining to thicken and thereby creating a nice, thick, squishy environment for a fertilised egg. If your progesterone levels are low or you have a history of early miscarriage, you may be prescribed a progesterone supplement in the form of a suppository.

And before you ask, you don't have to put it up your bum – any hole is a goal – but most women prefer bum to foofie because it is the more 'constrictive' of the two and leakage is minimal.

PRETERM PREMATURE RUPTURE OF THE MEMBRANES (PPROM) OR WATERS BREAKING EARLY

The amniotic sac (the bag of fluid your baby grows inside) usually bursts after thirty-seven weeks and indicates that labour is underway, but in around 3 per cent of pregnancies the amniotic sac breaks before thirty-seven weeks. It's like a wee that won't stop (a gush or a trickle) and it doesn't hurt, but it does increase the risk of infection. We don't know why waters sometimes break early – it might be caused by infection or placental problems – but if it happens you need to contact your midwife and go and get checked out as soon as possible.

What happens depends on how many weeks pregnant you are and your individual circumstances. It can't be 'fixed' once it's happened, but there are certain measures that can help:

- You may be given a short course of antibiotics to reduce the risk of an infection and delay labour.
- You may be given a course of steroid injections (corticosteroids) to help with your baby's development and to reduce the chance of problems caused by a premature birth.
- Once you are in labour, magnesium sulphate might be administered, which can reduce the risk of your baby developing cerebral palsy if it's a very premature birth.

RECURRENT MISCARRIAGE (RM)

RM is defined as having three or more miscarriages in a row. And it's f**king horrendous. There are thought to be a few main causes of RM and we have tried to list and explain them all here, but, as ever, there is a lot of extra information and advice on Tommy's website.

- Thyroid problems: these are sometimes linked to increased risk of pregnancy loss and other pregnancy complications.
- Thyroid antibodies: these little molecules in the bloodstream can attack the thyroid, causing it not to work properly. Having high levels of thyroid antibodies can increase the risk of miscarriage.
- Uterine problems: an abnormally shaped womb (see *Uterine abnormality*, page 272) can increase your risk of recurrent miscarriage and premature birth.
- Blood-clotting disorders: there are some rare disorders of the immune system (like systemic lupus erythematosus and antiphospholipid syndrome – or sticky blood) that affect the flow of blood to the placenta, which can prevent it from functioning properly, depriving baby of essential nutrients and oxygen.
- Genetic cause: in a small number of cases, one or both parents may pass on an abnormal chromosome, which can cause RM.
- Cervical weakness: if you have a history of late miscarriages and are considered at risk of having an *Incompetent cervix* (see page 261), you may be offered a scan from fourteen weeks to assess the length of your cervix.
- *Natural killer cells* (see page 265): some experts think that natural killer cells in the uterus play a part in infertility and miscarriage.

SPERM DNA FRAGMENTATION (SDF)

This is all about the quality of the swimmers. The higher the result, the more genetic abnormalities there are. It causes reduced fertility and increases the risk of miscarriage and IVF failure.

The biggie to know about here is that it's not routinely investigated. When a woman miscarries, the focus is on the female body initially.

If you had fertility problems and problems conceiving, male factors would be investigated but only with the focus on sperm count and motility. Recent research has shown that damage to the DNA that sperm carry can more than double the risk of miscarriage. F**kety f**k, f**k. And yet we (and we might be speaking just for ourselves now) knew zilch about this.

Causes of this fragmentation can include an infection, varicocele (like a varicose vein on the testes) or certain lifestyle choices like drinking or smoking, plus anything that can cause heat or friction in the nether regions – tight pants, cycling, sitting down all day, etc. BUT you can reduce SDF by:

- having a varicocele removed if there is one.
- avoiding alcohol and smoking.
- eating fresh foods and a balanced diet.
- avoiding all activities that could cause a warm atmosphere/ friction.

Plus, raising awareness of this – hell, putting a big friggin' spotlight on this! – will also, we're hoping, help.

SUBCHORIONIC HAEMATOMA (SCH)

A little something that rolls off the tongue, eh? Nope, but then again, this is a rare little something too. A SCH is bleeding between the membrane surrounding the foetus (the chorion) and the wall of the uterus. It affects around 1 per cent of all pregnancies and can be hard to pick up, as it doesn't always result in noticeable symptoms. Spotting or bleeding might well be a sign – often in the first trimester – but many subchorionic bleeds are detected during a routine ultrasound, without any noticeable signs or symptoms.

But what you really want to know is, how will it affect your pregnancy, right? First of all, a subchorionic bleed is a common cause of first-trimester bleeding and often occurs in uncomplicated pregnancies. They resolve themselves on their own and the majority of women go on to have normal and perfectly healthy pregnancies, because the SCH dissolves by itself.

BUT in rare cases, a SCH can cause the placenta to separate from the uterine wall, which may be linked to an increased risk of miscarriage or preterm labour. It is normal and healthy to worry when you notice vaginal bleeding or spotting during pregnancy, but remember that many SCH end in a healthy pregnancy. You'll be checked with ultrasounds until the haematoma reabsorbs itself (and you will get to see baby's heartbeat at every scan).

TERMINATION FOR MEDICAL REASONS (TFMR)

This four-letter acronym can't begin to explain the complications of such a baby loss. It is, in essence, the compassionate ending of a life and that is why many women like to call it compassionate induction instead. Many mothers think using the word 'termination' implies you have more choice than you realistically have in this situation, but please remember, this is just a medical term. The feelings you have if you are told you need to end your pregnancy are just as valid, as strong and as painful as those in any other type of baby loss.

You are likely to be offered a termination if your baby has been diagnosed with a condition that can cause death or serious disability. You might also be offered a termination if a pregnancy complication poses a serious risk to your own life. Both are incredibly traumatic experiences and there is an added guilt factor linked in with this because *you* will be making the decision. It's so important that you feel you have all the information you need before you decide. Your doctor/

healthcare worker/nurse are all valuable sources of information and can tell you more about the diagnosis and prognosis for each individual case. Take the time you need, get the support you need, and remember you have an inner strength and resolve that you won't think is possible. We are here for you.

TRANSVAGINAL ULTRASOUND SCAN

A transvaginal, or 'through the vagina', scan is when you get a lightsaber (or Wanda, as it's known across the pond) 'up your foofie'. Or, if we are being more specific, a small ultrasound probe with a sterile cover is passed into the vagina and images are transmitted onto a monitor.

These types of scans are used in early pregnancy, usually before 11 weeks, to give the clearest and most accurate picture of what is happening inside your uterus. You might be referred for one of these scans because of vaginal bleeding or spotting, or possibly because of problems in previous pregnancies. The internal examination isn't comfortable, but it isn't painful. It's safe and the best way to detect a baby's heartbeat.

The best time to have a scan is from about seven weeks, but you might be asked to return for another scan a week later if a heartbeat hasn't been detected – it could be that the baby is developing more slowly than expected or that the baby has died. Sometimes it can take several scans to know exactly what is happening and you will feel like you are in limbo, and the uncertainty of what is happening can be very stressful. Please find yourself some support if this happens to you.

UTERINE ABNORMALITY (UA)

There are several different abnormalities of the uterus and we are only covering them briefly here, so it's worth exploring them and checking out the diagrams available (Tommy's website has a good selection).

Each uterine abnormality can cause different problems with conception and in pregnancy. We've highlighted the variations in these problems under each heading and it's worth noting that women with UA might also have other conception or pregnancy difficulties, which might not be due to the UA itself. And you might not have any symptoms at all – you might only find out that there is an issue during gynae investigations. Phew! Right, here we go:

Bicornuate – heart-shaped womb
No difficulties with conception or in early pregnancy.

Slightly higher risk of later miscarriage and preterm birth and can affect the way the baby lies in later pregnancy (caesarean possibility).

Unicornuate – half the size of a normal uterus
This is rare.

No conception problems.

Increased risk of ectopic pregnancy, late miscarriage or preterm birth and can affect the way baby lies in later pregnancy (caesarean possibility).

Didelphic – double uterus, split in two
Each side will have its own 'cavity' (like, not the nicest term).

The duplication affects the uterus and cervix but can also affect the vulva, bladder, urethra and vagina.

No conception difficulties, but there's a small increase of preterm birth.

Septate – uterus split in two by a wall of muscle
Difficulties with conception.

Increased risk of first-trimester miscarriages and preterm birth.

Arcuate – a dip at the top of the uterus

No increased risk of preterm birth or first-trimester miscarriages.

Increased risk of second-trimester miscarriage and the need for a caesarean.

Resources

We hope you will be able to find lots of useful websites, links, social media pages and charities to follow on this page. We have mentioned about some of the campaigns and organisations in the book already, so this is the part where we try and be uber helpful by signposting the way to extra information.

TEMPLATE OF EMAIL FOR SCAN PHOTO

Please feel free to use the template below to help initiate the process of retrieving your baby scan photos. It might take a bit of chasing, or it might be dealt with swiftly, but we hope you'll find this useful as a starting point.

Good morning/afternoon,

I experienced a missed miscarriage – discovered on [add date]. At the time, I wasn't offered a scan picture, and in my distress I didn't ask for one. I know it's a long shot, but I was wondering if this was something you keep on record and, if so, whether I could obtain a copy.

I regret hugely not asking for a picture as it is the only memory I now have with my baby.

Thank you,
[Your name]

WEBSITES

We have mentioned some of these websites in the book, so fill your boots and follow the links for more info on each one.

- Not A Fictional Mum, Founder of the UK's first adoption and infertility brand and 'Make self-employed people eligible for statutory adoption pay', UK Government and Parliament Petitions: https://petition.parliament.uk/petitions/601323 www.notafictionalmum.com
- Sands United FC, a charity dedicated to supporting bereaved dads through a shared loved of sport: www.sands.org.uk
- Louisa MacInnes, certified Sex and Relationship coach expert offers her advice: www.louisamacinnes.com
- The Red Couch, the website where relationship expert Lilliana Gibbs explains more about the connections we have with ourselves and each other: www.theredcouch.co.uk
- The Grateful Hearts Club, where founder Charla Grant explains all about gratitude and what it looks like: www.thegratefulheartsclub.com
- Children with Cancer, a charity website that funds research and helps raise awareness about cancer in children: www.childrenwithcancer.org.uk
- Relax with Lucy & Co, a website dedicated to baby loss mindfulness and relaxation support: www.relaxwithlucy.co.uk
- Insight Timer, a free app to help with sleep, anxiety and stress: www.insighttimer.com
- The Ellie's Gift App is available to download from the Google Play app store
- Tommy's, a pregnancy charity that supports and champions people whatever their pregnancy journey may be: www.Tommys.org.uk

- In Memory of Lucas Alleebux, fundraising website in memory of Lucas: www.lucas-alleebux.muchloved.com
- NHS, Medical information on miscarriage and baby loss: www.nhs.uk
- Making Miracles, a baby trauma and family bereavement care website and charity: www.makingmiracles.org.uk
- Fight for IVF, Amber Izzo's campaign, is explained in lots of detail with ways in which you can support the initiative too: www.amberizzo.com/fight-for-ivf.com
- Miscarriage Association, a website packed full of information for those who have suffered miscarriage as well as friends, family and colleagues who want to help: www.miscarriageassociation.org.uk
- The Intended Parents Podcast, where Fran and Kreena share their journeys of infertility and surrogacy from the perspective of the girl next door. Available to listen on Apple Podcasts, Google and Spotify.

INSTAGRAM

Setting your preferences

Here is a tip to help get rid of all the crappy/triggering pregnancy and baby ads that you just don't need to see on your Instagram feed.

First, click on the three lines on the top right hand corner of your screen, then choose 'settings' then 'ads'. Now you are in 'ad topics' click on 'parenting' and then 'save'. We know it won't solve all your problems, but we hope it will help a little. Call us IT whizzes if you will, we like that.

A few Insta accounts that might be helpful when dealing with grief and are worth following (and which we blimin' love)

@themindfulgriefcoach
@pine_cones_and_study_days
@elliesgiftproject
@thegratefulheartsclub
@sandscharity
@notafictionalmum
@nicola.headley
@amber.izzo
@littlenorfolkcottage
@tfmrmamas
@ceci_fertilityhand
@the.infertile.midwife
@hannahpearn
@thefertilitymethod
@thisisalicerose

@fatpositivefertility
@tryingyears
@feathering_the_empty_nest
@bigfatnegative
@ruth_corden
@ihadamiscarriage
@definingmum
@iamlaurabradshaw
@bethfvank
@emmalcannon
@mummataralouise
@savlafaire
@loisgtransformationcoach
@ashascoli_poetry

KIDS' BOOKS

These are just a handful of some of the best picture books to read and share with young children to help them understand about matters ranging from sibling loss to adoption:

Badger's Parting Gifts by Susan Varley (Andersen Press, 1987).
The Invisible String by Patrice Karst (Little, Brown, 2018).
Robo-Babies by Laura Gallagher (Owlet Press, 2020).
Where Are You Lydie? by Emma Poore (Emma Poore, 2019).
These Precious Little People by Frankie Brunker (Independent Publishing Network, 2018).

The Blanket Bears by Samuel Langley-Swain (Owlet Press, 2019).

DOPPLERS

To use or not to use? THAT IS THE QUESTION...

Thinking of buying a doppler so that you can hear baby's heartbeat at home? This is a controversial topic. Have a read of some of the articles below so that you can make a more informed decision about this.

Information from the NHS on your baby's movements:

- Information from the NHS on your baby's movements: https://www.nhs.uk/pregnancy/keeping-well/your-babys-movements/
- Post from the charity Kicks Count, 'Why ditch the doppler?': https://www.kickscount.org.uk/why-we-want-home-doppler-sales-to-be-regulated
- Article from the Royal College of Midwifery, 'RCM advises pregnant women against use of dopplers': https://www.rcm.org.uk/media-releases/2020/january/rcm-advises-pregnant-women-against-use-of-personal-dopplers/
- Post from Tommy's, 'A word from us on home dopplers': https://www.tommys.org/pregnancy-information/blogs-and-stories/im-pregnant/tommys-midwives/word-us-home-dopplers

Index

Acknowledgements

There is absolutely no way we could have done this on our own. We have had support from many people along the way. Where do we even begin?

Thanks first to Abi, who helped us get this whole show on the road, from the initial call – 'Have you thought about writing a book?' – to filling in the gaps and taking the time to understand and echo our ethos.

Susan, thank you for sharing our 'big, ballsy' approach. Having you on our side has been instrumental for us and our message.

To Zoë and all at HQ for believing in the importance of this book, sharing our passion, bringing our much-loved project to fruition and being patient with us as we faffed around with fonts.

To our experts: Tahnee Knowles, Lucy Livesey, Louisa MacInnes, Charla Grant and Lilliana Gibbs – thank you for passing on your knowledge in order to help the recovery of others.

To the warriors – this community wouldn't exist without the wonderful warriors. Thank you for sharing your stories with us, for trusting us with your precious memories and for being a part of something so big and important: Not a Fictional Mum, Charla Grant, Clair Alleebux MBE, Frances Simmons, Chris Binnie, Sam Woolford, Jane Moscardini, Claire Hall, Noma Mzenda-Emego, Rhys and Leila King, Rebecca Plant, Laura Gallagher, Louise Taylor, Amber Izzo, Rebecca Dickson, Laura-Rose Thorogood, Dannika Agyeman, Hannah Foster and Sally Linghorn. To the MF Fellowship – Rachael, Becky, Georgie, Katie, Charlotte & Rebecca – thank you for helping us man the TWGGE lighthouse, giving us giggles and always having our backs. We love you all, short & tall.

BEX

Huge thank you to the most patient man in the world – my husband, Rob, for giving me the space and support I have needed to help build and maintain this incredible platform. You have given me all the time, love and kindness I could have wished for and, most importantly, recognised the importance of our work and my desire to help others. You've picked up so much slack for me in recent months without one complaint. I bloody loves ya.

Thank you, Mum, for the unwavering support, the pep talks and the constant reassurance. Thank you also for enabling me to reframe my experience when my world came crashing down. Thank you for consistently being my sounding board, my ego booster, my cheerleader and my gentle guide.

I am so lucky to have my wonderful children; since we started *TWGGE* I have realised what a miracle they truly are. I have kissed them harder and squeezed them tighter. James, Flynn, Ruby and my rainbow, Hazel.

Finally, to Laura. I've never met anyone like you before… In the year since we met, we've argued lots but laughed more. I am constantly in awe of your determination, your kindness and your capacity to help others. You are inspirational, and building this platform with you is my proudest achievement. Thanks for putting up with my endless passionate rants and ridiculous analogies. You are the anchor on HMS *TWGGE,* and you have all my love and my respect.

LAURA

A huge heartfelt thanks and heaps of gratitude go to all my family and friends, who have shown support and offered encouragement since we started *TWGGE*. From the pep talks and deep and meaningful chats to the more practical childcare and logistical support in everyday life, it's all helped me to be able to follow my passion to help others through the shittiest times of their lives.

It's been a tricky road – it still is; navigating our own journey while being fully immersed in this world of grief and loss has been tough, but we're muddling through. Thank you, Scoop, for your patience, love and understanding (most of the time). Without your grounding and support, it would be impossible to manage the work that we do. To Bertie, my miracle: I'll never know what it was that made you stick, but I know for certain that without you here I would not have the ability or strength to be able to do what I do.

To Bex: I can't believe that we only met in lockdown – it feels like forever that I have been listening to your passionate rants and airy-fairy analogies. At times I have felt like we've spent more time talking to each other than we have our families. I promise to continue to send you really interesting and long voice notes at ungodly hours. In all seriousness, I'm proud of us and all that we've created, and can't wait to see what the future holds for us all at *TWGGE*.

Special thanks also go to Rob (Number One employee of *TWGGE*).

ONE PLACE. MANY STORIES

Bold, innovative and
empowering publishing.

FOLLOW US ON:

@HQStories